ANIMAL CARE

FOURTH EDITION

Careers in Focus

ANIMAL CARE

FOURTH EDITION

Ferguson's
An Infobase Learning Company

Careers in Focus: Animal Care, Fourth Edition

Copyright © 2012 by Infobase Learning

All rights reserved. No part of this book may be reproduced or utilized in any form or by any means, electronic or mechanical, including photocopying, recording, or by any information storage or retrieval systems, without permission in writing from the publisher. For information contact:

Ferguson's
An imprint of Infobase Learning
132 West 31st Street
New York NY 10001

Library of Congress Cataloging-in-Publication Data

Careers in focus. Animal care. — 4th ed.
   p. cm. — (Careers in focus)
 Includes bibliographical references and index.
 ISBN-13: 978-0-8160-8037-3 (hardcover)
 ISBN-10: 0-8160-8037-2 (hardcover)
  1. Animal specialists—Vocational guidance—United States. 2. Animal culture—Vocational guidance—United States. I. J.G. Ferguson Publishing Company. II. Title: Animal care.
 SF80.C27 2011
 636.0023—dc23

2011016435

Ferguson's books are available at special discounts when purchased in bulk quantities for businesses, associations, institutions, or sales promotions. Please call our Special Sales Department in New York at (212) 967-8800 or (800) 322-8755.

You can find Ferguson's on the World Wide Web at http://www.infobaselearning.com

Text design by David Strelecky
Composition by Kerry Casey
Cover printed by Yurchak Printing, Landisville, Pa.
Book printed and bound by Yurchak Printing, Landisville, Pa.
Date printed: October 2011
Printed in the United States of America

10 9 8 7 6 5 4 3 2 1

This book is printed on acid-free paper.

All links and Web addresses were checked and verified to be correct at the time of publication. Because of the dynamic nature of the Web, some addresses and links may have changed since publication and may no longer be valid.

Table of Contents

Introduction

Animal care involves the care and maintenance of animals, both wild and domestic. The animal care field includes the training and breeding of animals, as well as promoting their health and care. It also includes the entire range of actions humans take to protect and preserve wildlife and ensure its continued survival, such as the regulation of hunting and fishing and the establishment of zoos and sanctuaries. Another important part of animal care is educating people about animals and their needs; for example, *naturalists* educate the public in a general way about animals and the environment, while *veterinarians* educate pet owners about specific concerns.

The animal care industry can be divided into two areas, although there are many jobs common to both. One area is the study and care of animals in the wild, which includes conservation, preservation of habitat, and research. The second area is the breeding and care of domesticated animals, including livestock, pets, and animals bred for sport and leisure.

People who study and care for fish and wildlife are generally well educated and highly experienced. *Biologists, zoologists,* and *ecologists* are some of the scientists who work in the field, in laboratories, wildlife refuges, museums, and zoos. They observe animals in the wild and in captivity to better understand their behavior—what they eat, how they mate, their social structure, how they defend against predators, how they raise their offspring, where they travel and how they interact with other animals and their environment. This helps scientists not only understand a particular species, but contributes to overall knowledge of the intricate living world, including human life. Knowledge about wildlife also helps scientists to be able to preserve natural habitats with hopes of preventing extinction of threatened species. Captive animals are also studied, as their behavior is altered by living in unnatural habitats and having to interact with and depend on humans. Some zoos and research facilities try as best they can to recreate as natural a habitat as possible, and some have programs for breeding threatened species in captivity with hopes of returning them to the wild.

Scientists are assisted by *zookeepers, breeders, technicians, photographers, park rangers, caretakers, administrators,* and other support workers with a wide variety of education and experience levels. Most positions in wildlife care are extremely competitive because of the large numbers of people interested in this field.

The care of domesticated animals also requires a wide variety of workers. The agricultural industry involves the care and handling of beef and dairy cattle, hogs, poultry, sheep, goats, and fish and shellfish. Jobs in this arena include *farmers, farm managers, agricultural technicians,* and *aquaculturists.*

Scientists and researchers are also involved with the care of farm animals, including experts in breeding, diet management, and the control of diseases and pests. They monitor meat and dairy quality and safety and develop vaccines and drugs to prevent viruses and bacteria. Some scientists develop new ways to use animals for human benefit besides food, for example, to provide vaccines, hormones, glues and resins, and other products. *Genetic scientists* have worked with farm animals for years, trying to develop breeds that are more resistant to disease, produce more milk or eggs, or produce meat that is leaner, for example.

Pet care is a rapidly developing industry in the United States, where new pet sitting and pet grooming businesses are opening all the time. Sixty-two percent of American households have one or more pets. According to the 2009–10 National Pet Owners Survey, it is estimated that Americans spend $47.7 billion a year on their pets, including food, veterinary care, grooming, and toys and supplies. Pet care businesses are becoming more regulated but still do not have very stringent certification or education requirements. They are open to enterprising animal lovers with good people skills and business sense. A new trend has been the opening of pet bakeries that make homemade biscuits and other treats for dogs and cats.

Pet care workers include those who need extensive training, such as *veterinarians* and *veterinary technicians. Breeders* and *trainers* need less rigorous training, but more experience. Positions that require little formal training or on-the-job training include *groomers, kennel workers, pet sitters, dog walkers,* certain positions at animal shelters, and *pet store workers.*

A number of domesticated animals are raised for sport and leisure. Equestrian management is big business, with 9.2 million domesticated horses in the United States. Those who work with horses include *farriers, horse breeders, horse trainers, jockeys, stable managers, riding instructors, ranch managers, racetrack managers, breeders,* and *groomers.* Horses are raised for racing, showing, and riding. They are the only animals that participate in the Olympics, in events such as dressage, show jumping, and cross-country jumping. Horses are also bred and trained for polo, rodeo, and police work.

The animal care industry in general is expected to grow over the next several years. Those occupations related to pets have an especially promising outlook, because pet ownership is on the rise and many owners are willing to invest substantial amounts of money in the care and grooming of their pets. The outlook for occupations related to the care of wild animals is less certain. Popular concern for wildlife is high, but public funding for park rangers and other wildlife caretakers is limited. Furthermore, competition for such jobs is very high and turnover is low, resulting in comparatively low salaries and few job openings. As in all fields, animal care jobs are always available for people with the right combination of education, experience, and determination; unlike many other fields, animal lovers can often create their own jobs.

Each article in this book discusses a particular animal care occupation in detail. The articles in *Careers in Focus: Animal Care* appear in Ferguson's *Encyclopedia of Careers and Vocational Guidance,* but have been updated and revised with the latest information from the U.S. Department of Labor, professional organizations, and other sources. The following paragraphs detail the sections and features that appear in the book.

The **Quick Facts** section provides a brief summary of the career including recommended school subjects, personal skills, work environment, minimum educational requirements, salary ranges, certification or licensing requirements, and employment outlook. This section also provides acronyms and identification numbers for the following government classification indexes: the Dictionary of Occupational Titles (DOT), the Guide for Occupational Exploration (GOE), the National Occupational Classification (NOC) Index, and the Occupational Information Network (O*NET)-Standard Occupational Classification System (SOC) index. The DOT, GOE, and O*NET-SOC indexes have been created by the U.S. government; the NOC index is Canada's career classification system. Readers can use the identification numbers listed in the Quick Facts section to access further information about a career. Print editions of the DOT (*Dictionary of Occupational Titles.* Indianapolis, Ind.: JIST Works, 1991) and GOE (*Guide for Occupational Exploration.* Indianapolis, Ind.: JIST Works, 2001) are available at libraries. Electronic versions of the DOT (http://www.oalj.dol.gov/libdot.htm), NOC (http://www5.hrsdc.gc.ca/NOC), and O*NET-SOC (http://www.onetonline.org/) are available on the Internet. When no DOT, GOE, NOC, or O*NET-SOC numbers are listed, this means that the U.S. Department of Labor or Human Resources and Skills Development Canada have not created a numerical designation for this career. In this instance, you will see the acronym "N/A," or not available.

The **Overview** section is a brief introductory description of the duties and responsibilities involved in this career. Oftentimes, a career may have a variety of job titles. When this is the case, alternative career titles are presented. Employment statistics are also provided, when available. The **History** section describes the history of the particular job as it relates to the overall development of its industry or field. **The Job** describes the primary and secondary duties of the job. **Requirements** discusses high school and postsecondary education and training requirements, any certification or licensing that is necessary, and other personal requirements for success in the job. **Exploring** offers suggestions on how to gain experience in or knowledge of the particular job before making a firm educational and financial commitment. The focus is on what can be done while still in high school (or in the early years of college) to gain a better understanding of the job. The **Employers** section gives an overview of typical places of employment for the job. **Starting Out** discusses the best ways to land that first job, be it through the college career services office, newspaper ads, Internet employment sites, or personal contact. The **Advancement** section describes what kind of career path to expect from the job and how to get there. **Earnings** lists salary ranges and describes the typical fringe benefits. The **Work Environment** section describes the typical surroundings and conditions of employment—whether indoors or outdoors, noisy or quiet, social or independent. Also discussed are typical hours worked, any seasonal fluctuations, and the stresses and strains of the job. The **Outlook** section summarizes the job in terms of the general economy and industry projections. For the most part, Outlook information is obtained from the U.S. Bureau of Labor Statistics and is supplemented by information gathered from professional associations. Job growth terms follow those used in the *Occupational Outlook Handbook*. Growth described as "much faster than the average" means an increase of 20 percent or more. Growth described as "faster than the average" means an increase of 14 to 19 percent. Growth described as "about as fast as the average" means an increase of 7 to 13 percent. Growth described as "more slowly than the average" means an increase of 3 to 6 percent. "Little or no change" means a decrease of 2 percent to an increase of 2 percent. "Decline" means a decrease of 3 percent or more. Each article ends with **For More Information,** which lists organizations that provide information on training, education, internships, scholarships, and job placement.

Careers in Focus: Animal Care also includes photographs, informative sidebars, and interviews with professionals in the field.

Animal Activists

OVERVIEW

Animal activists are advocates for animals. There are two main types of activists: *animal rights activists* and *animal welfare activists*. Animal rights activists work to protect the rights of animals, which for some organizations equal those of human rights. They believe animals should not be used as a source of food, clothing, entertainment, or medical experimentation. Some activists believe that animals should not even be kept as pets. Animal welfare activists accept the use of animals for the aforementioned purposes, as long as humane guidelines are followed. Animal activists work at the grassroots level to educate and organize the public, as well as lobby policy makers on behalf of animals.

HISTORY

Throughout history, certain people have objected to the way others have treated animals that were kept as pets, used in farming or other labor, or exhibited in zoos and aquariums. Some believed it was wrong to house wild animals in restrictive enclosures in zoos. Others believed it was wrong to raise animals for food. Some believed that it was okay to use animals for food and labor, and to keep them as pets, but that they should always be treated humanely.

One early animal activist was Henry Bergh, who founded the American Society for the Prevention of Cruelty to Animals (ASPCA). In 1863, Bergh was chosen by President Abraham Lincoln to represent the interests of the United States in Russia. During his time in Russia and other countries, he saw many people abusing animals.

QUICK FACTS

School Subjects
English
Speech

Personal Skills
Communication/ideas
Helping/teaching

Work Environment
Indoors and outdoors
Primarily multiple locations

Minimum Education Level
Varies by position

Salary Range
$19,540 to $37,790 to
$64,140+

Certification or Licensing
Required for certain
positions

Outlook
About as fast as the average

DOT
379

GOE
N/A

NOC
6463

O*NET-SOC
21-1099.00, 33-9011.00

Bergh felt this was wrong, and thought about ways to stop people from harming animals. This was not to say that the treatment of animals in the United States was any better. In Bergh's day, service animals such as horses and mules were beaten, starved, or allowed to suffer through blazing heat or frigid temperatures without any relief. People held dog and chicken fights to entertain crowds. Dogs were forced to pull street carts. In 1866, Bergh founded the ASPCA in New York City to provide, according to its Web site, "effective means for the prevention of cruelty to animals throughout the United States." He worked closely with business leaders and elected officials to educate people about the mistreatment of animals. Nine days after the ASPCA was founded, the New York state legislature passed an anticruelty law. The ASPCA was granted the legal right to enforce it. At the time of Bergh's death in 1888, 37 of the 38 states in the union had passed anticruelty laws.

In addition to the ASPCA, many other organizations have been formed to help protect the rights and welfare of animals, including the American Humane Association (1877), the Humane Society of the United States (1954), the World Society for the Protection of Animals (created in 1981 through the merger of the World Federation for the Protection of Animals and the International Society for the Protection of Animals), and People for the Ethical Treatment of Animals (1980). There are also thousands of organizations at the local and state levels.

THE JOB

When we wear leather shoes or fur-trimmed clothing, eat meat or seafood, are entertained at the circus, or purchase certain cosmetics, we often disregard the suffering of many different species of animals. Even many of the medicines and medical services we have at our disposal were created as a result of experimentation on animals. Animal rights activists vehemently oppose the use of animals for these purposes, and more. They believe that animals have rights equal to those of humans, and therefore should not be used as a source of food, clothing, entertainment, or medical experimentation.

Animal rights activists push for accommodation of the rights of animals, and believe that the public can, and should, change current customs, traditions, and industries in order to achieve these rights. The work of animal rights activists begins at the grassroots level by educating the public about the injustice of using animals for personal gain. Those working for People for the Ethical Treatment of

Animals (PETA), for example, may create campaigns based around a particular issue such as the slaughter of Canadian harp seals for their skins, the consumption of foie gras (duck livers), or the use of animals for experimentation.

Some animal rights organizations conduct direct action campaigns, some of which can cause damage to property, or even result in public disorder or violence. For example, the Animal Liberation Front (ALF) has been known to stage illegal direct action campaigns against animal rights offenders that have resulted in damages to research laboratories, kennels, and food processing companies. Members claim they believe in nonviolent tactics, yet in 2005 the U.S. Department of Homeland Security listed the ALF as a domestic terrorist threat. Other campaigns use attention-getting marketing plans, which some people view as extreme. One such example is PETA's antifur campaign, which posted billboards of nude models stating they "would rather go naked than wear a fur."

Animal welfare activists have a different view of animals than animal rights activists. Many support the use of animals for food, entertainment, clothing, experimentation, or other purposes as long as humane guidelines are followed. They often work for animal shelters and humane organizations that aim to ensure humane treatment of pets and farm animals.

Animal activists use a variety of methods to spread their message. They create literature and brochures to educate people about their beliefs. They prepare petitions and set up databases of concerned citizens and volunteers. Many campaigns include an action team that alerts members to developing news, upcoming events, and daily tips on how to improve the lives of animals. Activists may also organize demonstrations and rallies, sometimes traveling to the site to make sure the event is publicized and demonstrators are in place.

Animal activists use many cybertools to help in their campaigns. Social networking Web sites such as Facebook allow them to easily reach hundreds of thousands of "fans," or potential members. Some organizations' Web sites have links that visitors can use to apply for membership, make a donation, or contact their elected representative. PETA, for example, has links at its Web site for its different campaigns where members can fill out a petition online and send it directly to the targeted company's CEO or an elected official. Animal activists also use the Internet to post blogs or stream videos taken during undercover investigations of animal abuse.

Once a campaign has followers, it's up to the activist to make sure it gains momentum. They continue to send out information about the issue. They use mobile phone text messaging to alert members of new developments or causes. They talk to the press and spread their message using every possible means.

Animal activists come from a variety of backgrounds, each with skills that are important to their work. Those with technical skills may be assigned to help work on investigations. They review and transcribe investigators' notes, edit undercover videos, or log photos. They also maintain computer databases.

Activists with legal knowledge review evidence for possible law violations. They translate technical or legal documents into layman's terms for use in brochures, pamphlets, and press releases. They also participate in media interviews regarding a campaign, or represent the organization in court.

Some activists with a business background create action plans against those suspected of abusing animals for corporate gain. Some examples of major corporations targeted by PETA include McDonald's and Kentucky Fried Chicken's slaughtering methods used for cows and chickens, and Lowe's for selling glue traps (which cause captured animals to suffer before they die of thirst or starvation). Activists may prepare presentations to the corporations' CEOs or attend shareholder meetings to publicize their concerns and propose animal welfare changes. They may also hold news conferences.

Some animal activists work as *lobbyists,* who strive to influence legislation on behalf of a special interest group or a client.

There are several positions that can loosely be categorized under the heading of animal activist. *Humane investigators* (also known as *cruelty investigators* or *animal treatment investigators*) follow up on reports of animal neglect and abuse. They interview witnesses as well as animal owners who are accused of mistreatment. If the cruelty investigator determines that abuse or neglect exists, he or she may issue a warning, call the police to arrest the individual, or confiscate the animal. Humane investigators respond to reports of abandoned, stray, or injured animals, and they free-trap animals. They transport rescued animals to the shelter. *Humane educators* work at animal shelters and in the community teaching about humane treatment of animals and teach people about other animal-related issues. They travel to grade schools, high schools, clubs, and other community organizations. They lecture about animal rights, animal care and treatment, the overpopulation problem and potential solutions, the relationship between violence to animals and violence to people, and the roles of the individual and the community in effecting change. Humane educators arrange tours of the animal shelter for interested groups, distribute printed educational materials, and inform people about other resources for humane education.

REQUIREMENTS

High School
Many animal activists are college graduates, so in high school it is important to pursue a college preparatory curriculum that includes classes in mathematics, science, English, speech, computer science, social studies, and history.

Postsecondary Training
There are no minimum educational requirements to enter the field of animal activism, but many employers prefer that applicant's have a bachelor's degree. Activists possess a wide range of educational backgrounds, with many having degrees in animal science, animal behavior, or veterinary technology or science. Some activists have law degrees, while others earn degrees in veterinary medicine.

Animal rights and welfare lobbyists typically have an educational background in one of the aforementioned fields. The American League of Lobbyists (ALL) offers a certificate program for newcomers to the field as well as experienced practitioners who are seeking to hone their skills. Contact ALL for more information.

College-level courses in law enforcement, psychology, animal science, animal behavior, and veterinary technology could be useful for humane investigators. Humane investigators must be nominated by a humane organization for the special training required for certification.

Humane educators are often teachers. Although there are presently no degree requirements for this position, shelters are beginning to look for humane educators who have degrees in education and related fields. In addition, college or continuing education courses in psychology, public relations, and environmental education would be helpful to humane educators.

Certification or Licensing
Animal activists who work as lobbyists do not need a license or certification. They are required to register, however, as the Lobbying Disclosure Act of 1995 requires all lobbyists working at the federal level to register with the Secretary of the Senate and the Clerk of the House. Lobbyists may also be required to register with the states in

which they lobby and possibly pay a small fee. Lawyers, physicians, and humane investigators must be licensed.

Other Requirements

Animal activists must be committed to protecting the rights of animals. They should be energetic and have excellent communication skills. Other important traits for activists include knowledge of government and the legislative process; strong organizational skills; and a willingness to work long hours, including nights and weekends. They should also be able to stay calm and levelheaded when interacting with those who do not share their beliefs.

EXPLORING

Read publications about animal rights. Here are a few book suggestions: *Striking at the Roots: A Practical Guide to Animal Activism,* by Mark Hawthorne (O Books, 2007); *The PETA Practical Guide to Animal Rights: Simple Acts of Kindness to Help Animals in Trouble,* by Ingrid Newkirk (St. Martin's Griffin, 2009); and *Animal Rights,* by Christie Ritter (Abdo Publishing Company, 2008). Here are two magazine suggestions: *All Animals* (http://www.humanesociety.org/news/magazines/all_animals) and *Animal People* (http://www.animalpeoplenews.org).

Professional organizations can provide a lot of useful information about the field. For example, at the American Humane Association's Web site, http://www.americanhumane.org, you can learn about no-kill animal shelters; the association's Film & TV Unit, which monitors the treatment of animals used in entertainment; animal protections laws by state; and much more. At the Web site (http://www.aspca.org) of the American Society for the Prevention of Cruelty to Animals, you can learn about lobbying efforts to protect animals and types of animal cruelty such as dog fighting, puppy mills, horse and farm animal cruelty, and animal hoarding. Both organizations offer newsletters, e-mail alerts, and other publications; volunteer, internship, and employment options, and membership options for people who care about the protection of animals. The Humane Society of the United States (http://www.humanesociety.org), People for the Ethical Treatment of Animals (http://www.peta.org), and the World Society for the Protection of Animals (http://www.wspa-usa.org) offer similar resources at their Web sites. You can also read blogs, such as Encyclopaedia Britannica's Advocacy for Animals (http://advocacy.britannica.com/blog/advocacy). Finally, talk to an animal activist to learn more about what it's like to work in the field.

EMPLOYERS

Animal activists are employed by local, state, and national organizations that seek to protect the rights and ensure the humane treatment of animals. Opportunities are located throughout the United States, but are most frequently found in large urban areas. Many organizations only offer volunteer or part-time positions.

STARTING OUT

Many people land their first jobs in animal activism through contacts made during volunteer opportunities and internships. The organizations listed at the end of this article offer job opportunities, and the Humane Society of the United States offers job listings for other organizations at its Web site, http://www.humanesociety.org.

ADVANCEMENT

Animal activists can advance by working for larger organizations or starting their own group. Some activists run for elected office or work as congressional aides. Others work as college professors and authors.

EARNINGS

There is little salary information available for the career of animal activist. The U.S. Department of Labor reports that community and social service specialists (a category that includes animal activists) who worked for social advocacy organizations earned mean annual salaries of $37,790 in 2009. Salaries for all community and social service specialists ranged from less than $22,500 to $64,140 or more. Animal control workers, who investigate the mistreatment of animals, earned salaries that ranged from less than $19,540 to $51,170 or more in 2009.

Benefits for full-time workers include vacation and sick time, health, and sometimes dental, insurance, and pension or 401(k) plans. Self-employed workers must provide their own benefits.

WORK ENVIRONMENT

Animal activists work in a variety of employment settings. Some work in offices, while others spend a lot of time in the field investigating cases of animal abuse or exploitation, attending rallies and marches, teaching people about animal rights and welfare, or lobbying legislators about animal rights issues. Some activists work a typical 40-hour week, while others work many more hours, including at night and on weekends.

OUTLOOK

Employment for animal activists should remain steady during the next decade. Many people are concerned with protecting the rights and welfare of animals. Although this is good for animals, it makes it hard to land a full-time job in the field. Many jobs in animal activism are part time or volunteer in nature. Those with experience in the field and at least a bachelor's degree will have the best chances of landing a job.

FOR MORE INFORMATION

The association works to protect both children and animals.
American Humane Association
63 Inverness Drive East
Englewood, CO 80112-5117
Tel: 800-227-4645
E-mail: info@americanhumane.org
http://www.americanhumane.org

For information about a career as a lobbyist, contact the following organizations:
American League of Lobbyists
PO Box 30005
Alexandria, VA 22310-8005
Tel: 703-960-3011
E-mail: executivedir@alldc.org
http://www.alldc.org

American Society of Association Executives & Center for Association Leadership
1575 I Street, NW
Washington, DC 20005-1105
Tel: 888-950-2723
http://www.asaecenter.org

Women in Government Relations
801 North Fairfax Street, Suite 211

Alexandria, VA 22314-1757
Tel: 703-299-8546
http://www.wgr.org

For information on careers and training, contact
American Society for the Prevention of Cruelty to Animals
424 East 92nd Street
New York, NY 10128-6804
Tel: 212-876-7700
http://www.aspca.org

Visit the society's Web site for information on stopping animal cruelty.
Humane Society of the United States
2100 L Street, NW
Washington, DC 20037-1525
Tel: 202-452-1100
http://www.humanesociety.org

For information on how to get involved in animal activism, contact
People for the Ethical Treatment of Animals
501 Front Street
Norfolk, VA 23510-1040
Tel: 757-622-7382
http://www.peta.org

Visit the society's Web site to learn how to protect animals.
World Society for the Protection of Animals
Lincoln Plaza
89 South Street, Suite 201
Boston, MA 02111-2678
Tel: 800-883-9772
http://www.wspa-usa.org

Animal Breeders and Technicians

OVERVIEW

Animal breeders and technicians help breed, raise, and market a variety of animals: cattle, sheep, pigs, horses, mules, and poultry for livestock; pets such as canaries, parrots, dogs, and cats; and other more exotic animals such as ostriches, alligators, minks, and many zoo animals. Technicians who are primarily involved with the breeding and feeding of animals are sometimes referred to as *animal husbandry technicians*.

In general, animal breeders and technicians are concerned with the propagation, feeding, housing, health, production, and marketing of animals. These technicians work in many different settings and capacities. They may supervise unskilled farm workers; serve as field representatives assisting in the sales of animals to customers; work in kennels, stables, ranches, or zoos reproducing species and breeds for other clients or their own organization; or work on their own on a particular breed of interest. The diversity of employment available for well-trained and well-qualified animal breeders and technicians makes this career extremely flexible. As science progresses, opportunities for these technicians should broaden. Approximately 14,700 animal breeders are employed in the United States.

HISTORY

Breeding animals has been part of raising livestock since animals were first domesticated. With the discovery of genetics, the science behind the breeding selection became more exact. Great shifts can be made in a species with genetically selected breeding programs. All domesticated dogs extend from a precursor to the modern wolf. So even though miniature poodles and St. Bernards have extremely different appearances and are seemingly incompatible, they are actually so closely related genetically that they can reproduce with each other.

Farm animals have been bred to increase meat on the animal, increase production of eggs and milk, and increase resistance to disease. Both pets and farm animals have been bred for appearance, with show animals produced in almost every domesticated species.

As regions specialized in certain breeds, organizations developed to recognize and register them, eventually developing standards for accepted breeds. Organizations such as the American Kennel Club establish criteria by which species are judged, and the criteria can be quite specific. For example, dog breeds have specific ranges of height, shoulder width, fur color, arch of leg, and such, and any dog outside the variance cannot be shown in competition. This is partly to ensure that the species is bred by trained and informed individuals, and to keep the breed from inadvertently shifting over time. Breeds, however, can be intentionally shifted, and this is how new breeds begin.

Until the end of the 20th century, breeding was controlled by reproduction through mating pairs, whether through natural or artificial insemination. Recently, however, there has been a radical breakthrough in cloning, where the gene pool of the offspring remains identical to the parent cloned. Although this work is extremely costly and experimental, it is changing the range of work that breeders can do in reproduction.

THE JOB

Most animal breeders and technicians work as *livestock production technicians* with cattle, sheep, swine, or horses; or as *poultry production technicians,* with chickens, turkeys, geese, or ducks. Other animal breeders work with domesticated animals kept as pets, such as songbirds, parrots, and all dog and cat breeds. Even wildlife populations that are kept in reserves, ranches, zoos, or aquariums are bred with the guidance of a breeder or technician. Each category of animal (such as birds), family (parrot), species (African gray parrot), and even some individual breeds within a category have technicians working on their reproduction if they are bred for livestock or domestic use. Within each of these categories the jobs may be specialized for one aspect of the animal's reproductive cycle.

For example, technicians and breeders who work in food-source bird production can be divided into specific areas of concentration. In breeding-flock production, technicians may work as *farm managers,* directing the operation of one or more farms. They may be *flock supervisors* with five or six assistants working directly with farmers under contract to produce hatching eggs. On pedigree breeding farms, technicians may oversee all the people who transport, feed, and care for the poultry. Technicians in breeding-flock production seek ways to improve efficiency in the use of time, materials, and labor; they also strive to make maximum effective use of data-processing equipment.

Technicians in hatchery management operate and maintain the incubators and hatchers, where eggs develop as embryos. These technicians must be trained in incubation, sexing, grading, scheduling, and effectively using available technology. The egg processing phase begins when the eggs leave the farm. *Egg processing technicians* handle egg pickup, trucking, delivery, and quality control. With experience, technicians in this area can work as supervisors and plant managers. These technicians need training in egg processing machinery and refrigeration equipment.

Technicians in poultry meat production oversee the production, management, and inspection of birds bred specifically for consumption as meat. Technicians may work directly with flocks or in supervisory positions.

Poultry husbandry technicians conduct research in breeding, feeding, and management of poultry. They examine selection and breeding practices in order to increase efficiency of production and to improve the quality of poultry products.

Egg candlers inspect eggs to determine quality and fitness for incubation according to prescribed standards. They check to see if eggs have been fertilized and if they are developing correctly.

Some poultry technicians also work as *field-contact technicians,* inspecting poultry farms for food-processing companies. They ensure that growers maintain contract standards for feeding and housing birds and controlling disease. They tour barns, incubation units, and related facilities to observe sanitation and weather protection provisions. Field-contact technicians ensure that specific grains are administered according to schedules, inspect birds for evidence of disease, and weigh them to determine growth rates.

For other livestock, the categories are similar, as are the range of jobs. For nonfarm animals, the average breeder works with several animals within a breed or species to produce offspring for sale. Although there are ranches that produce a large number of exotic animals and some stables and kennels that run full-staff breeding operations, most breeders for pets work out of their homes. There are also production shops, usually referred to as puppy mills, that produce pets for sale but do so without much regard to the quality or well-being of the animals they are producing. Dismissed as unprofessional by established breeders and usually challenged by local authorities for quality of care provided to the animals, these are commonly not reputable enterprises, although they may be profitable in the short term.

One area of animal production technology that merits special mention because of the increasing focus on its use in animal husbandry is that of artificial breeding. Three kinds of technicians working in this specialized area of animal production are *artificial-breeding technicians, artificial-breeding laboratory technicians,* and *artificial insemination technicians.*

Artificial breeding can be differentiated by the goal of the breeder: food (poultry and cattle), sport (horses and dogs), conservation (endangered species kept in captivity), and science (mice, rabbits, monkeys, and any other animals used for research). Breeders work to create better, stronger breeds of animals or to maintain good existing breeds.

Because of the increasing cost of shipping adult animals from location to location to keep the gene pool diverse in a species or breed, animal breeders have developed successful methods of shipping frozen semen to allow breeding across distances.

Artificial-breeding technicians collect and package semen for use in insemination. They examine the semen under a microscope to determine density and motility of sperm cells, and they dilute the semen according to standard formulas. They transfer the semen to shipping and storage containers with identifying data such as the source, date taken, and quality. They also keep records related to all of their activities. In some cases they may also be responsible for inseminating the females.

Artificial-breeding laboratory technicians handle the artificial insemination of all kinds of animals, but most often these technicians specialize in the laboratory aspects of the activity. They measure purity, potency, and density of animal semen and add extenders and antibiotics to it. They keep records, clean and sterilize laboratory equipment, and perform experimental tests to develop improved methods of processing and preserving semen.

Artificial insemination technicians do exactly what their name implies: they collect semen from the male species of an animal and artificially inseminate the female. *Poultry inseminators* collect semen from roosters and fertilize hens' eggs. They examine the roosters' semen for quality and density, measure specified amounts of semen for loading into inseminating guns, inject semen into hens, and keep accurate records of all aspects of the operation. This area of animal production is expected to grow as poultry production expands.

Whether the breeding is done artificially or naturally, the goals are the same. *Cattle breeders* mate males and females to produce animals with preferred traits such as leaner meat and less fat. It is desirable to produce cows that give birth easily and are less susceptible to illness than the average cow. In artificial insemination, cows are inseminated with a gun, much like hens, which allows for many animals to be bred from the sperm of one male. By repeating the process of artificial breeding for many generations, a more perfect animal can be produced.

Animals raised for fur or skin also require extensive technological assistance. Mink farms, ostrich farms, and alligator farms are animal production industries that need husbandry, feeding, and health technicians. As the popularity of one species rises or falls, others replace it, and new animal specialists are needed.

For all breeders, it is essential that they keep track of the lineage of the animals they breed. The genetic history for at least three previous generations is usually considered the minimum background required to ensure no inbreeding. For animals sold as pedigreed, these records are certified by some overseeing organizations. For animals being bred from wildlife stock, purity of the genetic line within a breed or species is required before an animal is allowed to reproduce. Stud books list the lineage of all animals bred within a facility. Pedigree papers travel with an individual animal as a record of that animal's lineage. Both tools are essential to breeders to keep track of the breeding programs in operation.

There are several ways to decide which animals should be bred, and some or all of them weigh into the decisions that the animal breeders make. The physical appearance and the health of the animal usually come first; this is called mass selection—where the animal is selected of its own merits. If the animal has successfully reproduced before, this is called progeny selection. The animal can be bred again, knowing that the animal has produced desirable offspring previously. However, if that particular animal becomes genetically overrepresented in a generation, then the breeder runs the risk of inbreeding with the generations to follow. So the value of that animal's offspring has to be weighed against the need for diversity in parents. Family selection also determines the value of reproducing an animal. Some genetic diversity can come from breeding siblings of a good breeder, but it may not be enough diversity if the breeder is working with a limited stock of animals. Pedigree is the final determiner in evaluating a breeding animal.

REQUIREMENTS

High School
High school students seeking to enter this field will find that the more agriculture and science courses they select in high school, the better prepared they will be. In addition, courses in mathematics, business, communications, chemistry, and mechanics are valuable.

Postsecondary Training
Nine months to two years at a technical school or a college diploma are the usual minimum credentials for animal breeders and technicians. Many colleges now offer two- and four-year programs in animal science or animal husbandry where additional knowledge, skills, and specialized training may be acquired. Besides learning the scientific side of animal breeding, including instruction in genetics, animal physiology, and some veterinary science, students also take business classes that help them see the field from an economic point of view. With the increasing use of technology for breeding livestock and domesticated nonfarm animals, a bachelor's degree becomes more important for succeeding in the field. Master's and doctoral degrees are useful for the most specialized fields and the careers that require the most sophisticated genetic planning. Higher degrees are required for potential teachers in the field, and the current work being done in cloning is performed exclusively by people with doctorates.

Whether trained by experience, at an academic institution, or both, all new hires at major breeding companies are usually put through some type of training program.

Certification or Licensing
Certification is not required, but nearly all major companies have certification programs that can enhance earnings and opportunities.

Other Requirements
Animal breeders and technicians should have great love, empathy, and respect for animals. You must be patient and compassionate in addition to being very knowledgeable about the needs and habits of all the animals in your care. You must also have interest in reproductive science, genetics, and animal physiology. It is important to be

able to communicate easily with agricultural scientists, farmers, and other animal owners and caretakers.

EXPLORING

Organizations such as 4-H Clubs (http://www.4-h.org) and the National FFA Organization (formerly known as Future Farmers of America, https://www.ffa.org) offer good opportunities for hearing about, visiting, and participating in farm activities. Programs sponsored by 4-H allow students to learn firsthand about breeding small animals for show.

Other opportunities might include volunteering at a breeding farm or ranch, kennel, or stable where animals are bred and sold. This will give you a chance to see the work required and begin to get experience in practical skills for the job.

For at-home experience, raising pets is a good introduction to the skills needed in basic animal maintenance. Learning how to care for, feed, and house a pet provides some basic knowledge of working with animals. In addition, you can learn more about this field by reading books on animals and their care. But unless you have background and experience in breeding, and a good mentor to work with, it is not recommended that you start breeding your pet. There are literally millions of unwanted dogs and cats that come from mixed breeds or unpedigreed purebreds, and many of these animals are destroyed because there are no homes for them.

Other opportunities that provide animal maintenance experience include volunteering to work at animal shelters, veterinary offices, and pet breeders' businesses.

EMPLOYERS

Approximately 14,700 animal breeders are employed in the United States. Animal breeders and technicians used to work for themselves, but today most are employed by corporate breeders. A few may still own their own livestock ranches, and some do it only as a sideline or hobby.

STARTING OUT

Many junior colleges participate in "learn-and-earn" programs, in which the college and prospective employer jointly provide the student's training, both in the classroom and through on-the-job work with livestock and other animals. Most technical programs offer placement services for graduates, and the demand for qualified people often exceeds the supply.

ADVANCEMENT

Even when a good training or technical program is completed, the graduate often must begin work at a low level before advancing to positions with more responsibility. But the technical program graduate will advance much more rapidly to positions of major responsibility and greater financial reward than the untrained worker.

Those graduates willing to work hard and keep abreast of changes in their field may advance to livestock breeder, feedlot manager, supervisor, or artificial breeding distributor. If they have the necessary capital, they can own their own livestock ranches.

EARNINGS

Salaries vary widely depending on employer, the technicians' educational and agricultural background, the kind of animal the technicians work with, and the geographical areas in which they work. In general, the salaries of breeders tend to be higher in areas with a heavy concentration and in the breeding of certain specialty animals. Kentucky, for instance, leads the nation in the breeding of horses, and, unsurprisingly, that is where salaries are highest. The U.S. Department of Labor (DOL) reports that animal breeders earned mean annual wages of $29,680 in 2009. The top paid 10 percent made $60,390 or more, while the bottom paid 10 percent made $18,020 or less. Fringe benefits vary according to employer but can include paid vacation time, health insurance, and pension benefits.

WORK ENVIRONMENT

Working conditions vary from operation to operation, but certain factors always exist. Much of the work is done inside in all types of facilities. Barns, pens, and stables are the most common facilities for farm animals; nonfarm animals may be bred in private homes or housing facilities. Both types of work often require long, irregular hours and work on weekends and holidays. The work is also sometimes dangerous, especially when large animals such as stallions and bulls are involved. Salaries are usually commensurate with the hours worked, and there are usually slack seasons when time off is given to compensate for any extra hours worked. But for people with a strong desire to work with animals, long working hours or other less desirable conditions are offset by the benefits of this career.

Animal breeders and technicians are often their own bosses and make their own decisions. While this can be an asset to those who value independence, prospective animal breeders and technicians must realize that self-discipline is the most valuable trait for success.

OUTLOOK

Employment for animal breeders is expected to grow more slowly than the average for all careers through 2018, according to the DOL. Continuing changes are expected in the next few years, in both the production and the marketing phases of the animal production industry. Because of the costs involved, it is almost impossible for a one-person operation to stay in business for farm animals. As a result, cooperatives of consultants and corporations will become more prevalent with greater emphasis placed on specialization. This, in turn, will increase the demand for technical program graduates. Other factors, such as small profit margins, the demand for more uniform products, and an increasing foreign market, will result in a need for more specially trained personnel. This is a new era of specialization in the animal production industry; graduates of animal production technology programs have an interesting and rewarding future ahead of them.

FOR MORE INFORMATION

For information on careers and graduate programs, contact
American Society of Animal Science
2441 Village Green Place
Champaign, IL 61822-7676
Tel: 217-356-9050
E-mail: asas@assochq.org
http://www.asas.org

For industry information, contact
National Cattlemen's Beef Association
9110 East Nichols Avenue, #300
Centennial, CO 80112-3425
Tel: 303-694-0305
http://www.beef.org

For information on the agricultural industry, contact
U.S. Department of Agriculture
1400 Independence Avenue, SW
Washington, DC 20250-0002
Tel: 202-720-2791
http://www.usda.gov

Animal Caretakers

OVERVIEW

Animal caretakers, as the name implies, take care of animals. The job ranges from the day-to-day normal activities for a healthy animal to caring for sick, injured, or aging animals. Daily animal routine usually involves feeding and providing drinking water for each animal, making sure that their enclosure is clean, safe, appropriately warm, and, if needed, stocked with materials to keep the animal active and engaged. Caretakers may be responsible for creating different enrichment materials so that the animal is challenged by new objects and activities. They may exercise or train the animals. They may assist veterinarians or other trained medical staff in working with animals that require treatment. Animal caretakers may also maintain the written records for each animal. These records can include weight, eating habits, behavior, medicines given, or treatment given. Animal caretakers hold about 173,300 jobs in the United States.

HISTORY

The concept of raising, caring for, and medically assisting nonfarm or non-working animals is relatively new. The only animals, with few exceptions, that were kept by people were worked, such as plow-pulling oxen, or eaten, such as cattle, poultry, and pigs. The few examples of animals kept for pets are scattered accounts through history. The Egyptians kept cats as long ago as 3000 B.C.; cats were probably household pets, but

24

perhaps they were also for religious purposes. Until immunizations and pest control became common, though, keeping animals in the house was unwise for health reasons.

Over the thousands of years that people have kept animals for use, they have learned how to care for animals in captivity. Successful early farmers understood that animals needed them to provide food, shelter, and a healthy environment in which to live. From these early efforts, people have learned more specific methods of providing for animals' needs. But the idea to use these skills on animals that provide no labor or food was not accepted until nearly the 20th century.

The first institution that specifically focused on the humane treatment of animals was the Royal Society for the Prevention of Cruelty to Animals, founded in England in 1824. In the United States, the American Society for the Prevention of Cruelty to Animals (ASPCA) was founded in 1866. Nine days after the ASPCA was founded, the New York state legislature passed an anti-cruelty law. The ASPCA was granted the legal right to enforce it. But changes in animal treatment and rights were gradual throughout the first part of the 20th century. During the boom of the ecology movement in the late 1960s and early 1970s, public attention became focused on the rights and the needs of wildlife and domestic animals.

Rachel Carson's *Silent Spring* brought attention to the plight of hunting birds, and their rapidly deteriorating numbers. Pesticides such as DDT were dramatically reducing the population in the wild. To save birds such as the bald eagle, massive ecological intervention was required to clean up the environment, but breeding programs, shelters, and rescue centers would need to save individual birds to keep the population high enough to allow recovery.

Animals used in medical and chemical experimentation were also gaining advocates who helped create laws to protect them and begin to develop standards by which animals could be used in labs. As the public saw films and still pictures of the substandard or even abusive treatment of animals, particularly primates, in labs, they began to review treatment of animals elsewhere. Zoos, circuses, parks, and other institutions were used to replacing their animals with ones pulled from the wild. These institutions were soon under criticism about their pillaging of wild populations for healthy animals that wouldn't survive long in their care.

The institutions responded by improving facilities, nutrition, breeding programs, vaccination programs, and other forms of assistance that kept their animals healthier longer. Part of that improvement was increased staff. Also, as public interest in wildlife

Rabies: The Facts

- Rabies is a deadly disease caused by a virus that attacks the nervous system. Most often the virus is transmitted by a bite from a rabid animal.

- Proper treatment, administered promptly after being bitten, can stop the infection.

- In the United States, the majority of cases of rabies have occurred in humans following close exposure to a bat—without any signs or recollection of a bite.

- Not all rabid animals foam at the mouth and appear mad; infected animals can appear tame and calm.

- Only mammals get rabies; birds, fish, reptiles, and amphibians do not.

- Cats are the most common domestic animal to become infected with rabies; this is attributed to the fact that many cats are not vaccinated but are exposed to rabid animals while outdoors.

- Most cases of rabies occur in wild animals, primarily bats, skunks, raccoons, and foxes.

increased, there was an increase in the pool of volunteers that these institutions could draw on for labor.

With the push to conserve and protect species and maintain the populations in captivity and in the wild, programs such as re-release programs for injured animals, rescue programs for threatened populations, zoo breeding programs, pet breeding and care programs, and sanctuary land for wild populations became much more prevalent. Many of these programs began and continue to be staffed by advocates, volunteers, and professionals who can all be called animal caretakers.

Finally, the horse industry provides a consistent source of work. In some areas, such as Kentucky, Oklahoma, and California, horses are a huge industry. Horses, though legally considered farm animals, occupy a strange middle ground between pets and livestock. Some, such as carriage horses or cow horses, are working animals. Others, such as dressage horses, polo ponies, and hunter/jumpers, are valued for their athletic potential, and can, at least in theory, be trained and then sold for a higher price, or bred and their offspring sold for a tidy profit. Yet others are strictly pleasure and companion animals.

THE JOB

Animal caretakers, also referred to by several other names depending on their specialty, perform the daily duties of animal care, which include feeding, grooming, cleaning, exercising, examining, and nurturing the individuals in their care. These caretakers have titles such as *animal shelter workers, grooms, veterinary assistants, wildlife assistants, animal shelter attendants, laboratory animal technicians, laboratory animal technologists,* and *kennel technicians.*

Animal caretakers are employed in kennels, stables, pet stores, boarding facilities, walking services, shelters, sanctuaries, rescue centers, zoos, aquariums, veterinary facilities, and animal experimentation labs. They may also be employed by the federal government, state or local parks that have educational centers with live animals, the Department of Agriculture in programs such as quarantine centers for animals coming into the United States, and the Centers for Disease Control laboratories.

Almost every one of these employers expects the animal caretaker to provide the daily maintenance routine for animals. The caretaker may be responsible for one animal or one species, or may be required to handle many animals and many species. A veterinary assistant is likely to encounter dogs and cats, with the occasional bird or reptile. A *wildlife shelter worker* works with the local wild population, so for much of the United States that means working with raccoons, skunks, porcupines, hunting birds, songbirds, the occasional predator such as coyote or fox, and perhaps large animals such as bear, elk, moose, or deer.

Caretakers are responsible for some or all of the following tasks: selecting, mixing, and measuring out the appropriate food; providing water; cleaning the animal and the enclosure; changing bedding and groundcover if used; moving the animals from night facilities to day facilities or exercise spaces or different quarters; sterilizing facilities and equipment not in use; recording and filing statistics, medical reports, or lab reports on each animal; and providing general attention and affection to animals that need human contact.

The animal caretaker learns to recognize signs of illness such as lack of appetite, fatigue, skin sores, and changed behavior. They check the animals they can physically approach or handle for lumps, sores, fat, texture of the skin, fur, or feathers, and condition of the mouth. Since most animals do not exhibit signs of illness until they are very ill, it is important that the caretaker who sees the animal most regularly note any small change in the animal's physical or mental state.

The caretaker also maintains the animal's living quarters. For most animals in their care, this will be an enclosure of some type. The enclosure has to be safe and secure. The animal should not be able to injure itself within the enclosure, be able to escape, or have outside animals able to get into the enclosure. Small holes in an enclosure wall would not threaten a coyote, but small holes that a snake can pass through could threaten a rabbit. Horses can injure themselves in their stables, and in addition are vulnerable to a multitude of pasture injuries.

The quarters need to be the right size for the animal. If they are too large, the animal will feel threatened by the amount of open space, feeling it cannot protect the area adequately. Inappropriately small enclosures can be just as damaging. If the animal cannot get sufficient exercise within the enclosure, it will also suffer both psychologically and physically.

Caretakers set up and oversee enrichment activities that provide the animal with something to keep it engaged and occupied while in its home. For even the smallest rodent, enrichment activities are required. Most of us are familiar with enrichment toys for our pets. These are balls and squeaky toys for dogs and cats, bells and different foot surfaces for birds, and tunnels and rolling wheels for hamsters and gerbils. Wild animals require the same stimulation. Animal caretakers hide food in containers that require ingenuity and tools to open (ideal for a raccoon), or ropes and inner tubes for animals such as primates to swing on and play with.

Animals that can be exercised are taken to specially designed areas and worked. For hunting birds this may mean flying on a creance (tether); for dogs it may mean a game of fetch in the yard. Horses may be lunged (run around), or hacked (ridden); they may also simply be turned out in a field to exercise themselves, but some form of training is useful to keep them in optimal riding condition. Domestic animal shelters, vet offices, kennels, boarding facilities, and dog-walking services work predominantly with domesticated dogs and cats, and perhaps horses at boarding centers. Exercise often consists of walks or free runs within an enclosed space. The animal caretaker for these employers often works with a rotating population of animals, some of whom may be in their care only for a few hours or days, although some animals may be cared for over longer periods. Caretakers at sanctuaries, quarantines, laboratories, and such may care for the same animals for months or years.

It is also an unpleasant side of the job that in almost every facility, the caretaker will have to deal with the death of an animal in his or her care. For veterinary offices, shelters, and wildlife facilities of any type, animal deaths are a part of everyone's experience. Shelters may choose to euthanize (kill) animals that are beyond medical treatment, deemed unadoptable, or unmaintainable because of their condition or the facilities' inability to house them. But even for places without a euthanasia policy, any center working with older, injured, sick, or rescued animals is going to lose the battle to save some of them. For the animal caretaker, this may mean losing an animal that just came in that morning, or losing an animal that he or she fed nearly every day for years. It can be as painful as losing one's own pet.

As an animal caretaker gains experience working with the animals, his or her responsibilities may increase. Caretakers may begin to perform tasks that either senior caretakers were performing or medical specialists were doing. This can include administering drugs; clipping nails, beaks, and wing feathers; banding wild animals with identification tags; and training the animal.

There are numerous clerical tasks that may also be part of the animal caretakers' routine. Beyond the medical reports made on the animals, animal caretakers may be required to screen people looking to take an animal home and write status reports or care plans. The animal caretaker may be responsible for communicating to an animal's owner the status of the animal in his or her care. Other clerical and administrative tasks may be required, depending on the facilities, the specific job, and the employer. But for most animal caretakers, the day is usually spent looking after the well-being of the animals.

REQUIREMENTS

High School

Students preparing for animal caretaker careers need a high school diploma. While in high school, classes in anatomy and physiology, science, and health are recommended. Students can obtain valuable information by taking animal science classes, where available. Any knowledge about animal breeds, behavior, and health is helpful. The basics of human nutrition, disease, reproduction, and aging help to give a background for learning about these topics for different species. A basic grasp of business and computer skills will help with the clerical tasks.

Postsecondary Training

There are two-year college programs in animal health that lead to an associate's degree. This type of program offers courses in anatomy and physiology, chemistry, mathematics, clinical pharmacology, pathology, radiology, animal care and handling, infectious diseases, biology, and current veterinary treatment. Students graduating from these programs go on to work in veterinary practices, shelters, zoos and aquariums, pharmaceutical companies, and laboratory research facilities. Students should look for programs accredited by the American Veterinary Medical Association.

Apprenticing for the handling of wild hunting birds is required by most facilities. This can include having apprentices pursue a falconry license, which means apprenticing to a licensed falconer.

A bachelor's degree is required for many jobs, particularly in zoos and aquariums. Degrees in wildlife management, biology, zoology, animal physiology, or other related fields are most useful.

Certification or Licensing

As mentioned earlier, caretakers who handle wild hunting birds may need to have a falconry license, which means apprenticing to a licensed falconer. Certification for assistant laboratory animal technicians, laboratory animal technicians, and laboratory animal technologists is available from the American Association for Laboratory Animal Science and may be required by some employers.

Other Requirements

Animal caretakers should have great love, empathy, and respect for animals. They should have a strong interest in the environment. Patience, compassion, dependability, and the ability to work on repetitive, physically challenging, or unstimulating tasks without annoyance are essential characteristics for someone to be happy as an animal caretaker.

EXPLORING

Volunteering is the most effective method of experiencing the tasks of an animal caretaker. Most shelters, rescue centers, and sanctuaries, and some zoos, aquariums, and labs rely on volunteers to fill their staff. Opportunities as a volunteer may include the ability to work directly with animals in some or all of the capacities of a paid animal caretaker.

There is always a concern, sometimes justified, that an organization will never pay someone whose services they have gotten for free. You may not be able to get paid employment from the same organization for which you volunteered. But many organizations recognize the benefit of hiring prior volunteers: they get someone who already knows the institution, the system, and the preferred caretaking methods.

Volunteering also provides a line on your resume that demonstrates that you bring experience to your first paying job. It gives you references that can vouch for your skills with animals, your reliability, and your dedication to the field. Thus, you should treat any volunteer position with the same professionalism that you would a paid job.

Other avenues for exploration are interviewing people already in the position, or finding a paid position in a facility where animal caretakers work so you can see them in action. You may also begin by providing a pet walking or sitting service in your neighborhood, but be sure to only take on the number and kinds of animals you know you can handle successfully.

EMPLOYERS

Approximately 173,300 nonfarm animal caretakers are employed in the United States. There are many different types of facilities and businesses that employ animal caretakers, including veterinary offices, kennels, stables, breeding farms, boarding facilities, rescue centers, shelters, sanctuaries, zoos, aquariums, and pet stores. Other job opportunities for animal caretakers are provided by the government and state and local parks. This field is growing, and increasing job opportunities will be available all over the country for animal caretakers. Since pet ownership and interest in animals continues to increase, more and more jobs will become available with all kinds of employers, resulting in work in environments ranging from nonprofit organizations to retail stores to laboratories.

STARTING OUT

High school students who volunteer will be able to test the job before committing to it. They will also, as explained earlier, be able to get a job on their resume that demonstrates their experience in the field.

Two- and four-year college programs offer some placement assistance, but familiarity with the regional market for organizations that use animal caretakers will assist you in selecting places to target with your resume. Many animal caretakers work in veterinary offices and boarding facilities or kennels, but animal research laboratories also hire many caretakers. Other employers include the federal government, state governments, pharmaceutical companies, teaching hospitals, and food production companies.

ADVANCEMENT

Advancement depends on the job setting. There may be promotion opportunities to senior technician, supervisor, assistant facilities manager, or facilities manager. Some animal caretakers may open their own facilities or services. Services such as dog walking require little in the way of offices or equipment, so these are easy ways for animal caretakers to start on their own, with an established clientele that they bring from a previous position.

Laboratory workers can move from assistant technician to technician to technologist with increased education and experience. But for most promotions, more education is usually required.

EARNINGS

Salaried animal caretakers earned an average salary of $19,550 in 2009, according to the U.S. Department of Labor (DOL). The top paid 10 percent earned more than $31,660, and the bottom paid 10 percent earned less than $15,590 a year.

Self-employed animal caretakers who provide dog walking, kennel, sitting, or other cottage industry services do not have salaries that are readily available for review, but in large cities, boarding a dog overnight can cost $25 to $110, with a minimum of three dogs usually at one facility. Dog walkers charge between $8 and $20 a dog for a 30-minute visit. There is little overhead for either service, beyond perhaps providing food.

Benefits for full-time workers include vacation and sick time, health, and sometimes dental, insurance, and pension or 401(k) plans. Part-time workers must provide their own benefits.

WORK ENVIRONMENT

Animals may either be kept indoors or outdoors, in any type of weather. Eagles do not come in from the rain, so animal caretakers caring for eagles still have to traipse outside to feed them when it's raining. Horses are turned out in the middle of the winter, so horse grooms still have to carry bales of hay to the pasture in the middle of January snowdrifts. Though currying, saddling, exercising, medicating, and cleaning up after a horse—or horses—may seem like a dream job to some, it is considerably less romantic to clean a stable day in and day out, regardless of weather.

Depending on the facilities, heavy lifting may be part of the job. You may have to lift crates, animals, food, equipment, or other items big enough to accommodate a large animal. The work can sometimes be hard, repetitive, and dirty. Cleaning enclosures and disinfecting spaces can involve hot or cold water and chemicals.

The work can also be dangerous, depending on the animals you work with. Although animals that are handled correctly and are treated with the proper respect and distance can be quite safe, situations can arise where the animal is unpredictable, or is frightened or cornered. Although this is more likely with animal caretakers working with wildlife populations, large dogs, horses, and cattle are quite capable of injuring and killing people. There is a certain physical risk involved in working with animals, which may be as minor as scratches from nails or bites, but can be as great as broken or crushed bones, or accidental death.

Many facilities require long workdays, long workweeks, odd hours, weekend work, holiday work, and intermittent schedules. Depending on the hours of the facility, the services provided, and the staffing, there may be several shifts, including a graveyard shift. Animal caretakers should be prepared to work a changing schedule. The needs of animals don't cease for weekends and holidays.

Also, for many facilities, animals that require round-the-clock care have to be taken home with an animal caretaker who is willing to provide whatever service the animal needs, including waking every two hours to bottle-feed a newborn chimp.

OUTLOOK

The animal care field is expected to grow much faster than the average for all careers through 2018, according to the DOL. More people have pets and are more concerned with their pets' care. Since most households have all the adults in full-time employment, animals are left home alone longer than in earlier times. Dog-walking services, pet sitting and in-house care, boarding facilities, kennels, and such that provide assistance with the daily care of an animal for the working or traveling owner are far more prevalent and successful than before.

Veterinary services are also on the rise, with the increased number of pets and the increased awareness on the part of owners that vet services are essential to an animal's well-being.

There is a high turnover in the profession. This is due in part to the seasonal nature of some of the jobs, the low pay, and the lack of advancement opportunities in the field. Wildlife sanctuaries, release and rescue programs, shelters, and zoos and aquariums are heavily dependent on charitable contributions and fund-raising efforts. Staff employment can be tied to the rise and fall of donations. Many of these institutions rely heavily on volunteer labor. As such, the competitiveness for the paid jobs is quite high.

Positions as animal caretakers in zoos, aquariums, and rehabilitation and rescue centers are the most sought after, partly because of the ability to work with exotic and wild species. Aspiring animal caretakers will find few openings in these facilities.

Graduates of veterinary technician programs have the best employment prospects. Laboratory animal technicians and technologists also have good opportunities. Increasing concern for animal rights and welfare means that these facilities are staffing more professionals to operate their labs.

FOR MORE INFORMATION

For information about animal laboratory work and certification programs, contact
American Association for Laboratory Animal Science
9190 Crestwyn Hills Drive
Memphis, TN 38125-8538
Tel: 901-754-8620
E-mail: info@aalas.org
http://www.aalas.org

For more information on careers, schools, and resources, contact
American Veterinary Medical Association
1931 North Meacham Road, Suite 100
Schaumburg, IL 60173-4360
Tel: 800-248-2862
http://www.avma.org

For information on available training programs, such as the facility accreditation program, certification program for kennel operators, complete staff training program, and ethics program, contact
Pet Care Services Association
401 North Michigan Avenue, Suite 220
Chicago, IL 60611-4255
Tel: 800-218-9123
http://www.petcareservices.org

Animal Handlers

OVERVIEW

Anybody who works directly with animals, from the *caretaker* of your local park's petting zoo, to the *wildlife biologist* who reintroduces wild animals to national parks, is an *animal handler.* Animal handlers care for, train, and study animals in such places as zoos, parks, research laboratories, animal breeding facilities, rodeos, and museums. An animal handler's job involves feeding the animals, cleaning their living and sleeping areas, preparing medications, and other aspects of basic care. A handler may also be actively involved in an animal's training, and in presenting animals to the public in shows and parks. Approximately 173,300 nonfarm animal care and service workers are employed in the United States.

HISTORY

From the old stable hand of the 19th-century Wild West to today's horse trainer for a movie western, animal handlers have long been in great demand. As long as animals have walked the earth alongside humans, society has invented ways to use animals for work, recreation, and research. Ancient Egyptian records of veterinary medicine date as far back as 2000 B.C. Animal medicine was considered as important as human medicine, because of the great importance animals played in transportation and production. But animals weren't just admired for their practicality; people have always held affection and fascination for animals. The domestication of animals began during the Stone Age, and zoo keeping can be traced back to the 12th century B.C.

Egypt, Greece, and China all have early records of exotic animals kept in collections for admiration and competition. Though many of the earliest zoos were kept only for kings and queens, public zoos have been in existence for over two centuries. The French Revolution resulted in the Jardin de Plantes in Paris going public and becoming a model for all the zoos to follow as monarchies fell around the world.

With the development of engines and motors over the last century, the role of animals in society has changed. Though seeing-eye dogs, laboratory primates, police horses, and canine patrol dogs are still put to work to aid humans, animals today entertain and fascinate more often than perform duties. Protecting animals has become an important aspect of every animal handler's job. For nearly 150 years, nonprofit agencies have been in place to ensure the humane treatment of animals. The first such agency in the United States was the American Society for the Prevention of Cruelty to Animals. It was chartered in 1866 and is still active today.

THE JOB

Wrangling an iguana for a movie production, preparing the diet for a zoo's new albino alligator, comforting bison to keep them from committing "suicide," training cats for an animal-assisted therapy program at a nursing home—all these responsibilities, strange as they may seem, actually exist for some animal trainers. Many western states have long telephone book listings of animal handlers who rent out trained iguanas, horses, cougars, cattle, and other animals for movie productions. Zoos and marine animal parks hire highly trained keepers to feed, shelter, and protect some of the most exotic animals in the world. Bison, if not properly prepared for transport, can easily be provoked to stampede, sometimes killing themselves. And even cats are therapists these days, as people introduce their pets to elderly and ill patients who respond well to interaction with animals.

Whether taking on jobs like those listed above or working for a small park or large zoo, all animal handlers are called upon for the daily care and safety of animals. They may have special training in a particular animal or breed or work with a variety of animals. With a wide knowledge of an animal's nutritional and exercise requirements, animal handlers make sure the animals in their care are well fed, well groomed, and healthy. They prepare food and formulas, which may include administering medications. Maintaining proper shelters for animals requires cleaning the area,

How Much Does an Elephant Eat?

In the wild, of course, elephants graze on vegetation—about 500 pounds of it in a day. Elephants in zoos and circuses, however, have to be fed by their handlers. An elephant eats the following:

- About six-and-a-half pounds of bran, mixed with water and minerals, for breakfast
- 55 pounds of hay
- 22 pounds of straw
- 30 pounds of turnips, carrots, or other vegetables
- Nine pounds of bread
- About 20 pounds of fruits and vegetables several times a week
- As many tree branches as he or she wants!

ensuring good ventilation, and providing proper bedding. Animal handlers arrange for vaccinations, as well as look for diseases in their animals. They also prepare animals for transport, knowing how to use muzzles and kennels, and how to calm an animal. But an animal handler needs a rapport with the two-legged creatures as well; working with people is an important aspect of most animal care jobs, as many of these animals are kept for presentation and performance.

The relationship between an animal and its handler can be very strong, particularly in training situations. Dogs trained for a police unit require specially certified trainers, and the dogs often both live and work alongside the officers to whom they are assigned. The same is true of handlers who train seeing-eye dogs or hearing-ear dogs; it is the handler's responsibility to train the animal to think of itself and its owner as one unit, thereby assuring it will watch out for both its own safety and that of its owner. Handlers who breed animals are often very devoted to the animals they place in other homes—they often interview prospective buyers, making sure the animal will have proper shelter, exercise, and feeding. Handlers who prepare animals for research in a lab must pay close attention to animal health, as well as their own; many states require health tests and immunizations of people who run the risk of catching diseases or illnesses from the animals they study.

REQUIREMENTS

High School

Take biology, chemistry, and other science courses offered by your high school. The study of science will be important to any student of animals, as will the study of psychology and sociology. Knowing about animal nutrition, health, behavior, and biology will help you to understand the animals you care for, and how to best provide for them. And if you do choose to go on to college, most animal-related courses of study are science based.

Some may think of animal handlers as people who spend all their time separate from the rest of the community, communicating only with animals and limiting interaction with humans. However, nothing could be further from the truth—most animal handlers work actively with the public; they present the animals in zoos and public programs, and may even perform with the animals. Join your speech and debate team, or your drama club, to prepare for speaking in front of groups of people.

Because so many animal programs, from petting zoos to animal-therapy programs, rely on community support, there are many volunteer opportunities for high school students looking to work with animals. Zoos, parks, and museums need volunteers, as do kennels, shelters, and local chapters of the Humane Society of the United States (or the Humane Society of Canada). These organizations may even offer students paid part-time positions. If few opportunities exist in your area, check with the nearest zoo about summer internship programs for high school students.

Postsecondary Training

The value of a college degree depends on the work you do. Many animal handlers do not have degrees, but zoos often prefer to hire people with a postsecondary education. A degree can often determine promotions and pay raises among the workers of a zoo. Many universities offer degrees in animal sciences, zoology, and zoological sciences. There are also graduate degrees in zoology, which may require courses in physiology, animal behavior, and oceanography. Courses for animal science programs generally focus on animal research, but some programs allow students to create their own course plans to involve hands-on experience as an animal handler. Santa Fe Community College in Gainesville, Florida, offers a unique and popular wild animal technology program; students work toward an associate's degree while gaining a great deal of first-hand zoo experience. The students run a 65-species zoo entirely on their own and, upon graduation, enter bachelor's programs or other animal care jobs.

Some consider a job as an animal handler an internship in and of itself; after gaining experience in a petting zoo or teaching zoo, or working with a breeder or stable hand, some animal handlers pursue careers as zookeepers, veterinarians, and animal researchers. Most college animal science and zoology programs offer some hands-on experience with animals; in the case of the Santa Fe Community College, an internship with the school's zoo is required along with the academic classes.

Many unpaid internships are available for those willing to volunteer their time to researchers and other animal professionals. Check with your local university and zoo to find out about opportunities to study animals in the wild, or to reintroduce animals to their native habitats.

Certification or Licensing

Some animal handlers in very specialized situations, such as patrol dog trainers and lab animal technicians, are required to pursue certification. The American Association for Laboratory Animal Sciences offers certification for those working with lab animals. But for the majority of animal handlers, no certification program exists. Accreditation is generally only required of the institutions and programs that hire animal handlers. The American Zoo and Aquarium Association offers accreditation, as well as memberships to individuals. Though members are required to have a certain amount of experience, membership is not mandatory for those working with animals.

Other Requirements

It is important for animal handlers to love the animals they care for. What might not be as apparent, however, is the need for animal handlers to enjoy working with people as well. Animal handlers are often required to present the animals to park and zoo visitors, and to serve as tour guides; they also work as instructors in zoo and museum education programs. Some animal handlers even perform alongside their trained animals in theme parks and shows. Some shows, such as marine animal shows, can be particularly strenuous, calling for very athletic trainers.

Working with animals on a daily basis requires patience and calmness since animals faced with unfamiliar situations are easily frightened. Animal handlers must be very knowledgeable about the needs and habits of all the animals in their care. Handlers are often called upon to transport animals, and they must know ways to best comfort them. Impatience may result in serious injury to both the animal and the handler.

EXPLORING

If you grew up with a family pet or have spent time on a farm, you're probably already very familiar with how to care for animals. But if you want to gain experience handling a large group of animals, contact your local zoo about volunteer or part-time positions. Many zoos have programs in place to introduce young people to the duties and responsibilities of an animal handler. If your local zoo doesn't have such a program, try to create your own: contact zookeepers, express your interest in their work, and ask to "shadow" them for a few days.

Many part-time jobs are available to high school students interested in working with animals. Pet shops, petting zoos, stables, and kennels are likely to have a few after-school positions. In larger cities, you may be able to start your own animal care business as a dog walker or pet sitter. Or look under "animal handler" in the local telephone book. Some animal handlers work exclusively with movie production crews and other entertainment venues; you may be able to work as a temporary assistant on a production.

EMPLOYERS

Animal handlers are employed by zoos, aquariums, parks, animal shelters, movie studios, research laboratories, animal breeding facilities, rodeos, and museums. There are about 173,300 nonfarm animal care and service workers in the United States.

STARTING OUT

Depending on the area of animal care in which you want to work, you may be able to find many great opportunities. A high school job or internship is a good start; experience with animals is what is most important to employers hiring handlers. Any volunteering you've done will also look good to an employer because it shows that you have a personal dedication to the care of animals. Kennels, petting zoos, museums, and animal shelters often run classified ads in the newspaper; due to the lower pay and some of the hazards involved in handling animals, those positions are frequently available.

Jobs with zoos in major cities, or with animal shows, can be highly competitive. If you're hoping to work in a larger, more famous zoo, you should first pursue experience with a smaller zoo. Jobs working with marine mammals are also difficult to get; because there are few marine animal shows in the country (such as those performed at Sea World parks), you may first have to pursue experience with internships and college programs.

ADVANCEMENT

Most people who work with animals are not looking to climb any ladder of advancement. As a matter of fact, many people change from high-paying careers to lower paying animal care jobs just to do something they love. Some who have gained experience handling and training animals may start their own businesses, perhaps building their own stables of trained "actors" to hire out for area movie shoots, stage shows, parades, and other performances. Some animal handlers may pursue higher education while working full or part time, taking courses toward veterinary sciences degrees, or degrees in biology. With a degree, an animal handler may have a better chance at the higher paying, supervisory zookeeper positions. After years with a particular zoo, an animal handler can take on more responsibility and make decisions that influence the direction of the zoo.

EARNINGS

The opportunity to work directly with a variety of different animals is often reward enough for animal handlers. Someone who owns a stable of well-trained animals used in performances may be able to negotiate for large contracts, or a successful dog breeder may make a comfortable living with an established business, but most animal handlers make do with small salaries and hourly wages. Santa Fe Community College advises new graduates of its animal technology program to expect between $20,000 and $23,000 annually. This wage varies according to region—in the colder Midwestern and Northern states, and in California, animal handlers can make more than those living in the Southeast. The U.S. Department of Labor estimates that nonfarm animal caretakers earned a median salary of $19,550 in 2009, with 10 percent earning less than $15,590 and 10 percent more than $31,660. Many full-time, salaried zoo positions include health insurance and paid vacation and sick days, among other benefits.

WORK ENVIRONMENT

Depending on the lives of the animals for which they care, handlers usually work both indoors and outdoors. But the indoors is often nothing more than an animal shelter, and not much different from the pens outdoors. Be prepared for smelly, messy, and dusty environments; if you have allergies, they'll be under constant assault. It will be both to your benefit, and the animal's, to make sure you work in well-ventilated areas. Some institutions, particularly animal research labs, require handlers to have immunizations and physicals before working with the animals. In addition to allergies, there is some danger of diseases transferred from animals to humans. These risks can be lessened with protective clothing like lab coats, gloves, and ventilated hoods.

The temperament of your animals will also affect your work environment. Handlers must be prepared for occasional scratches, bites, and kicks from animals with even the best dispositions. Though some animals can be very noisy when disturbed, handlers attempt to keep their animals' surroundings quiet and calm.

OUTLOOK

With the popularity of cable channels such as the Discovery Channel and Animal Planet, as well as television specials and videos featuring animals, the public's interest in animals is only likely to increase. Zoos, parks, and museums will benefit a great deal from any increased exposure the public has to the animal kingdom. Zoos must also compete with television as family entertainment, and therefore are constantly thriving to improve their facilities with more exotic animals, better shelters, and more programs to involve the public directly with animals.

Concerns about the treatment of animals will perhaps lead to more stringent laws and certification requirements. Some activists hope to end the capture of animals for display in zoos; some even object to filming animals in the wild. But zoos will likely continue to operate and expand, with zoo professionals arguing that zoo animals are often safer and receive better care than they would in their natural habitats.

FOR MORE INFORMATION

For general information about zoos, aquariums, oceanariums, and wildlife parks, contact
Association of Zoos and Aquariums
8403 Colesville Road, Suite 710
Silver Spring, MD 20910-3314
Tel: 301-562-0777
http://www.aza.org

For information on its wild animal technology program, contact
Santa Fe Community College
3000 NW 83rd Street
Gainesville, FL 32606-6210
Tel: 352-395-5600
http://www.sfcollege.edu/zoo

Animal Shelter Employees

OVERVIEW

Animal shelter employees work in non-profit organizations. Their duties are similar to those performed in animal control agencies, which are run by government entities—city, county, state, or federal. Animal shelters and animal control agencies differ in their purpose and philosophy. Animal shelters, also called humane shelters, are usually dedicated to the protection of animals and the promotion of animal welfare. Animal control agencies exist to ensure that the safety and welfare of people and property are not compromised by animals. In recent years, animal shelters and animal control organizations have increasingly been working together. Some animal control organizations maintain shelter facilities or take animals to shelters for care and adoption.

Animal shelter employees perform a variety of jobs related to the welfare and protection of domestic animals. Most shelter workers care for small domestic animals, such as cats, dogs, and rabbits, but employees at some shelters may also work with horses, goats, pigs, and other larger domestic animals. Sick and injured wild animals are usually cared for by wildlife refuges and wildlife rehabilitation centers, not animal shelters.

HISTORY

The precursors of today's animal shelter employees were the pound masters of the colonial United States. In the early 1700s, animal

Cruelty to Animals

According to the American Humane Association, violence toward animals results from the same causes as violence toward humans. Research indicates the following:

- Young people who are cruel to animals are more likely to become aggressive toward humans.
- Most prisoners who are incarcerated for violent crimes abused animals during childhood.
- Children who learn cruel behaviors from adults may imitate them on animals.
- Children abuse animals to release the aggression they feel toward abusive adults.

pounds were built to house stray animals. Pound masters kept the strays until their owners claimed them. Animals that were not claimed were drowned or otherwise destroyed. In the 18th and early 19th centuries, the treatment of animals in the United States was frequently harsh and even cruel.

The American Society for the Prevention of Cruelty to Animals was founded in 1866 through the efforts of philanthropist Henry Bergh and other early crusaders for animal welfare. It was the first organization of its kind in the United States. Not long after, Caroline Earle White and the Women's SPCA of Pennsylvania founded the first truly humane animal shelter. These two events brought into existence the position of animal shelter worker as we know it today. As a result of these developments, the focus of animal shelter employees turned from animal control toward a greater concern for the welfare and humane treatment of animals.

The job of animal shelter employee took on another dimension in the middle of the 20th century. Greater emphasis was placed on training shelter workers in better techniques of caring for animals, and better methods for humanely euthanizing (killing) animals were developed.

New positions for animal shelter workers are evolving as we move further into the 21st century. Shelter employees focus on reuniting lost pets with their owners, adoption efforts, and humane education, volunteer, and community outreach programs. Studies now show that there is a strong link between violence toward animals and violence toward people. Environmental groups are educating the public about the interrelationships among plants, animals, people, and the planet as a whole. As public awareness of animals' importance and connection to mankind grows, the work of animal shelter employees will continue to evolve.

THE JOB

The duties of shelter employees range from cleaning cages and grooming animals to education, fund-raising, and business management. The functions a specific worker performs frequently depend on the size of the animal shelter. In a large shelter, duties are more specialized, and there may be a large staff to accomplish them. In a small shelter, a few individuals may be responsible for nearly all of the functions that are performed. Whatever the specific duties of an animal shelter worker may be, the goal is always to promote the welfare of animals. The following paragraphs detail some of the more common career paths at animal shelters.

Kennel attendants (also called *kennel workers*) generally tend to the animals' physical needs, such as feeding, exercising, and cleaning of living quarters. Of all shelter staff, the kennel attendants work most closely with the shelter animals, and an important part of their job is nurturing the animals through caring handling. In some shelters, kennel attendants receive animals that are brought in by their owners or by a humane investigator. The *receiving attendant* may be responsible for checking the general health of the new animal, finding an appropriate habitat for it in the shelter, and referring it for medical treatment when necessary. Kennel attendants keep records, such as the identification of the animal, size, weight, and general condition. More experienced or skilled kennel attendants may be trained to give some inoculations and perform euthanasia under the supervision of a veterinarian. (In larger shelters, a worker with special training called a *euthanasia technician* may perform euthanasia.) Kennel attendants sometimes act as adoption counselors.

Adoption counselors screen applicants who wish to adopt animals from the shelter. They interview applicants to ascertain whether they will provide a good, caring home for an animal. An adoption counselor asks questions, listens carefully, communicates tactfully with people, and judges character. If the counselor decides the applicant is a good potential pet owner, he or she must try to match the qualified owner with an appropriate animal. If the adoption counselor believes a proposed adoption would not be in the animal's interest, the application is denied. A skilled counselor may be able to suggest a different animal that would be a better match for the applicant's situation. The adoption counselor puts the animal's welfare foremost, but also promotes the public image of the shelter.

Humane investigators (also known as *cruelty investigators* or *animal treatment investigators*) follow up on reports of animal abuse and neglect. They interview any witnesses as well as animal owners who are accused of mistreatment. If the cruelty investigator determines that abuse or neglect exists, he or she may issue a warning, call the police to arrest the individual, or confiscate the animal. Humane investigators respond to reports of abandoned, stray, or injured animals, and they free-trap animals. They transport rescued animals to the shelter.

Humane educators work at the shelter and in the community teaching about humane treatment of animals and raising awareness of other animal-related issues. They travel to grade schools, high schools, clubs, and other community organizations. They lecture about animal care and treatment, animal rights, the overpopulation problem and potential solutions, the relationship between violence to animals and violence to people, and the roles of the individual and the community in effecting change. Humane educators arrange tours of the animal shelter for interested groups, distribute printed educational materials, and inform people about other resources for humane education. *Shelter managers* (also called *kennel managers* or *kennel supervisors*) oversee all the daily operations of the shelter itself. They hire and train kennel attendants, make schedules for staff and volunteers, evaluate work performance, and provide continuing education opportunities to improve job performance. Shelter managers supervise and/or perform the maintenance of the property, buildings, vehicles, and euthanasia equipment. In some shelters, the manager is responsible for operating the euthanasia equipment when animals must be destroyed according to shelter policy.

Shelter administrators are responsible for the overall operation of the shelter, its departments, and its programs. They select and hire shelter managers, humane educators, humane investigators, and department heads, and they may be in charge of personnel. Administrators advocate for the shelter by holding interviews with the media, fund-raising, attending community events, and recruiting new members. Shelter administrators must work well with people, and they must be good business managers. The majority of animal shelters that fail in the United States are forced to close because they were not run like businesses. Some larger organizations have both an executive director and an administrative director who divide the administrative duties.

Other career options include veterinarian, veterinary technician, customer care manager, behavior coordinator, human resources manager, secretary, and receptionist.

REQUIREMENTS

High School

Kennel attendants and adoption counselors usually need a high school diploma or GED certificate. Some shelters hire high school students who are legally of age to work and who show an aptitude for working with animals and with the public. High school classes in biology and other sciences help prepare students for working with shelter animals. English, speech, debate, and drama classes can help develop the self-confidence and verbal skills needed for interaction with the public and for interviewing adoption candidates. Mathematics, business, and computer courses build a foundation for the record-keeping and business-management aspects of these positions—and for promotions. (These high school courses would also be of value to any employee in an animal shelter.) Most training is done on the job, and most promotions are made from within. Volunteering at a local shelter, kennel, or veterinary hospital is an excellent way to gain experience in this field while still in high school. Owning and caring for a pet and reading about animals, their care, and related topics can also be helpful.

Postsecondary Training

Many states require some college and special certification from humane investigators. College-level courses in law enforcement, psychology, animal science, animal behavior, and veterinary technology could be useful for humane investigators. Humane investigators must be nominated by a humane organization for the special training required for certification.

Humane educators are often teachers. Although there are presently no degree requirements for this position, shelters are beginning to look for humane educators who have degrees in education and related fields. In addition to the high school courses recommended for kennel workers, college or continuing education courses in psychology, public relations, and environmental education would be helpful to humane educators.

Shelter managers are frequently required to have a college degree, but experienced kennel workers who do not have degrees can be promoted into this position. Veterinary technicians or managers of other types of kennels might also be considered for a shelter manager position. An individual who hopes to become a shelter manager would be well advised to take college or continuing education courses in business management, veterinary technology, animal management, or animal husbandry.

Shelter administrators generally need a bachelor's degree or strong experience in business management or shelter management. Some executive director positions may even require a master's degree. Helpful areas of study include business administration and management, finance, public relations, fund-raising, grant writing, negotiations, and personnel development.

Educational requirements for other shelter workers vary by position. For example, veterinarians need a medical degree, while veterinary technicians must have a minimum of an associate's degree in veterinary technology. Customer care managers may need some postsecondary training or prior experience in customer service. Behavior coordinators learn their skills by attending community colleges and vocational schools that offer courses and workshops in animal training. Human resources managers often have associate's or bachelor's degrees in human resources management or business.

Certification or Licensing
The position of humane investigator requires licensing in some states. The Society of Animal Welfare Administrators offers voluntary certification for animal welfare administrators. No other certification or licensing is available for animal shelter workers at this time. No labor unions are associated with the field.

Other Requirements
To make a good animal shelter worker, two of the most important ingredients are a respect for people and a love of animals. Animal shelter employees must work well with people in order to effectively promote the welfare of animals. They must be able to work independently and at the same time be good team players. They must be patient, compassionate, dedicated, organized, and hard working. Animal shelter workers need to be good communicators and good decision makers. Rachel Hendricks started her animal welfare career giving preliminary exams and doing lab work for the Community Animal Rescue Effort at the Evanston Animal Shelter in Evanston, Illinois. She summed up the requirements for

A facility manager walks a dog through a shelter. (*Greg Eans, AP Photo*/The Daily Reflector)

an animal shelter employee: "You have to work together. You have to love doing it. You get your rewards from the animals. It has to be in your heart."

EXPLORING

Public libraries have excellent books that give a detailed look into the world of animal shelters and humane societies. Many of the major national associations maintain Web sites that offer a variety of information and resources. Individuals who want to learn more about animal shelter work should contact a local shelter to inquire about humane education presentations that are scheduled in the community. They might attend humane education sessions or an open house at the shelter.

After some preliminary research, an individual might ask to interview a kennel worker or volunteer in order to learn about the position. Some shelters might agree to allow an interested person to spend a day following or working with a kennel worker.

Volunteering at a shelter is the best way to learn how you would like a career as an animal shelter employee. Animal shelters welcome volunteers who are considering a career in the field.

EMPLOYERS

Read books about animal shelter careers. Here is one suggestion: *One at a Time: A Week in an American Animal Shelter,* 3d edition, by Diane Leigh and Marilee Geyer (No Voice Unheard, 2005). Animal shelters exist all over the country, and an increasing interest in the treatment and welfare of animals points toward growing numbers of shelters. Larger shelters may employ workers in a variety of positions, whereas smaller shelters may depend on a few workers managing a number of responsibilities. Small shelters and shelters in rural areas can rarely offer much beyond retirement plans and health insurance in the way of benefits, and often they have only part-time positions available. Larger shelters in metropolitan areas, on the other hand, can sometimes offer attractive benefits packages, plus opportunities for advancement within the organization. Since animal shelters are nonprofit organizations, their survival depends on their continued ability to raise the funds required to operate.

STARTING OUT

The best way to get started in the field is to volunteer. Shelters depend heavily on volunteers, and loyal volunteers are first to be given an opportunity when a paid position opens. Most volunteers, like most animal shelter workers, start out as kennel workers and/or adoption counselors. The skills learned in those positions provide the basis for advancement. A helpful aspect of beginning a career as an animal shelter employee is that it is possible to enter the field from many backgrounds. A teacher might become a humane educator. A public health official could become a humane investigator. Business professionals and accountants could become shelter managers, administrators, or executive directors. It takes many skills to successfully run an animal shelter, and each individual can apply his or her expertise to improving the shelter and enhancing the welfare of the shelter animals.

ADVANCEMENT

For animal shelter employees, most opportunities for advancement come from within. Since few formal training programs exist, on-the-job training provides the majority of learning and advancement opportunities. The national associations, such as the American Humane Association and the Humane Society of the United States, publish training materials and sponsor training programs throughout the country. As animal shelter workers learn more and become more skilled, they are often promoted from one position to another. A good kennel attendant might be given the opportunity to study to become a humane investigator. An experienced kennel attendant, adoption counselor, humane investigator, or humane educator could eventually become a shelter manager. A shelter manager might become a shelter administrator. A shelter administrator may eventually become executive director of an organization. Any animal shelter employee who is interested in gaining a different position can study to acquire the skills needed for that position and work to acquire the experience.

In some cases, advancement may depend on the size of the shelter. Small shelters offer opportunities for employees to learn many skills, but they may not offer many avenues for advancement. Large shelters have more positions and more opportunities for advancement, but they may not provide the opportunity to learn as many skills at one time. Individuals may need to be willing to relocate to find a better chance for growth. Local animal shelters and newspaper listings are good places to look for local job openings. The national associations are good sources of information on job openings throughout the country.

EARNINGS

There is a wide range of salaries and benefits for animal shelter employees. Some differences depend on the size and location of the shelter. Large shelters in metropolitan areas generally offer higher pay and more benefits. Small shelters and those in rural areas may offer lower salaries, and some may only provide part-time employment.

According to the U.S. Department of Labor, median annual earnings of nonfarm animal caretakers were $19,550 in 2009. Salaries ranged from less than $15,590 to more than $31,660.

Entry-level kennel workers and adoption counselors often start at minimum wage. They earn around $15,080 a year if they work full time. With experience and training, salaries for these positions increase. Animal control workers earned salaries that ranged from less than $19,540 to $51,170 or more in 2009, with a median of $40,720.

Salaries for senior managers range widely based on the size of the facility. Managers at small facilities earn from $20,000 to $40,000, while those employed at large facilities earn $25,000 to $100,000 or more a year. Executive directors earn between $20,000 and $150,000.

Most shelters offer at least a health insurance benefit, though some may not. Some health insurance plans require that the employee contribute a part of the monthly premium. Shelters offer retirement plans. Some of the larger shelters and associations have very attractive benefit packages.

WORK ENVIRONMENT

Animal shelter employees have the moral satisfaction of promoting the welfare of animals. They feel joy and pride because they make a difference in the lives of animals and people. They may also experience sadness and anger at the suffering they witness among the animals that are sick, injured, or abused. In some shelters, suffering or unadoptable animals are euthanized. Animal shelter employees may be upset when this is necessary. Individuals who are philosophically or emotionally opposed to euthanasia can choose to work in no-kill shelters where the animals are kept until they are adopted.

For most animal shelter employees, schedules and hours of work vary. In smaller shelters, and even in some larger ones, everyone—including the executive director—may be involved in the care and feeding of the animals. If the work is not done at the end of an eight-hour day, it must be completed. Most shelters are staffed 24 hours a day every day of the year. Weekend, evening, and holiday work is often required.

Shelter kennel attendants have the pleasure of working closely with the animals. This can be enjoyable and satisfying. Kennel workers wear comfortable, casual clothes, which many employees consider a benefit. Most of the work is inside the shelter, but animals are sometimes exercised outside. Keeping animals and their habitats clean is physically demanding. Kennel workers lift and move heavy animals, cages, and bags of feed. They also have to bend and stoop to work with animals and clean cages. Kennels are often noisy and sometimes have strong or unpleasant odors. Workers may be exposed to hazardous chemicals in cleaning agents. They may be bitten, scratched, or kicked by animals. Some workers may be allergic to animals. The work can be repetitive, but the animals themselves provide variety.

Adoption counselors also work closely with the animals. They get to know the personalities of the animals so they can try to match each animal with an appropriate home. Counselors work mostly indoors. They work in the kennel area and in the office. Many shelters provide private rooms where the counselors meet with adoption applicants. Depending on the philosophy of the shelter and their other duties, adoption counselors may dress casually or in office attire. Since they work with the public, adoption counselors may experience stress when dealing with unpleasant, angry, or unreasonable people.

Humane investigators work indoors and outdoors. Their clothing may be casual, or they may wear uniforms. Their duties are physically demanding. They have to run, climb, crawl, or swim to catch strays or rescue trapped or injured animals. They may be hurt by animals that feel threatened. They may also be exposed to rabies and other communicable diseases carried by the animals they rescue. Confronting individuals accused of animal neglect or abuse can be stressful and even dangerous. Humane investigators may be on call for emergencies; weekend and evening work is likely.

Humane educators usually work indoors. They dress in casual or office attire, depending on their schedule and other duties. They frequently travel around the community. Humane educators from larger shelters may travel around the state or country. Their work involves the stress of dealing with the public, and they frequently have deadlines for developing materials and presentations.

Shelter managers work indoors and outdoors. They work in an office and in the shelter kennels. Their attire can vary depending on the philosophy of the shelter and the work they are performing on a given day. They may be exposed to hazardous chemicals. They may experience stress due to supervising volunteers and employees and dealing with the public.

Shelter administrators work mostly indoors in quiet offices. Most dress in professional attire, but those who also work in the kennels may dress more casually. Administrators travel to community events and meetings, and they may travel for fund-raising purposes. They can experience a high degree of stress related to financial matters, business management, and public relations.

OUTLOOK

According to the Humane Society of the United States and the American Humane Association, the United States is in a serious pet overpopulation crisis. According to the American Pet Products Association, there were 77.5 million dogs and 93.6 million cats in U.S. households as of 2009. In theory, a single female cat and her offspring can produce 420,000 cats in seven years; in six years, a single female dog and her offspring can produce 67,000 dogs. Despite early spay/neuter programs and the concerted efforts of shelters and veterinarians to reduce the problem, the overpopulation is expected to continue into the foreseeable future. While 3 to 4 million cats and dogs are adopted from shelters each year, a roughly equal number have to be euthanized. Therefore, employment of animal caretakers in kennels and animal shelters should remain steady. Turnover is often high among kennel workers due to the strenuous physical work, generally low-income level, and the often-heavy emotional strain. As a result, the availability of jobs should be good for those workers.

At middle-management and upper-management levels, jobs will keep pace with those of entry-level positions due to the increasing number of shelters and types of positions within them.

There is increasing awareness of the plight of domestic animals and wildlife throughout the world. This suggests that the outlook should be very good for the future for those interested in animal shelter and welfare work at the international level.

FOR MORE INFORMATION

The American Humane Association works to protect both children and animals. Its Web site lists current job opportunities in animal protection and provides links to other animal welfare organizations.

American Humane Association
63 Inverness Drive East
Englewood, CO 80112-5117
Tel: 800-227-4645
E-mail: info@americanhumane.org
http://www.americanhumane.org

The American Society for the Prevention of Cruelty to Animals provides training programs for shelter workers. Its Web site details its services and provides links to other humane organizations' Web sites.

American Society for the Prevention of Cruelty to Animals
424 East 92nd Street
New York, NY 10128-6804
Tel: 212-876-7700
http://www.aspca.org

The Humane Society of the United States advocates for animals, the earth, and the environment. Its Web site has educational articles, details the organization's goals, and provides links to other humane organizations.

Humane Society of the United States
2100 L Street, NW
Washington, DC 20037-1525
Tel: 202-452-1100
http://www.humanesociety.org

The association "promotes professionalism in the animal protection care and humane law enforcement field." Visit its Web site for information on careers and publications.

National Animal Control Association
PO Box 480851
Kansas City, MO 64148-0851
Tel: 913-768-1319
E-mail: nca@ncanet.org
http://nacanet.org

Visit the society's Web site for information on certification and job listings.

Society of Animal Welfare Administrators
15508 West Bell Road, Suite 101-613
Surprise, AZ 85374-3436
Tel: 888-600-3648
E-mail: admin@sawanetwork.org
http://www.sawanetwork.org

The World Society for the Protection of Animals (WSPA) is made up of more than 900 humane societies from 150 countries. Its primary focus is developing animal protective programs at the government level. WSPA serves as the international "Red Cross" for animals in need anywhere in the world.

World Society for the Protection of Animals (WSPA)
Lincoln Plaza
89 South Street, Suite 201
Boston, MA 02111-2678
Tel: 800-883-9772
http://www.wspa-usa.org

INTERVIEW

David Miller is the executive director of the Peggy Adams Animal Rescue League of the Palm Beaches in West Palm Beach, Florida. He discussed his career with the editors of Careers in Focus: Animal Care.

Q. How long have you worked in the field? Why did you choose to enter this career?

A. I have worked in the animal welfare industry for a total of 14 years. I worked in the for-profit world directly after college. It wasn't until I met someone from the Humane Society of Broward County, Ft. Lauderdale, who was looking to reorganize the organization's structure to be more like a for-profit center, that I became involved in this industry. A lot of my responsibilities at my job were exactly what they were looking for at Broward County. This was my first contact with the industry.

I've always loved animals, always grown up around animals. It was unique to think this could be a career for me—something I could do as a full-time job. The more I got involved, and the more people I met around the country that were involved in animal welfare, I asked myself, "How could I not work in animal welfare?"

As a business administration major in college, I received a well-rounded education. Looking back, I am thankful for the degree that I have because it has given me good exposure to a lot of different areas of business. Running a business and running a nonprofit has a lot of similarities—we fund-raise, we try to market ourselves just like any other business, we have expenditures we have to control, and an operation we need to run. I really think my major is well suited for the job I do.

Q. What are the pros and cons of your job?

A. This is an emotional mission. The euthanasia rate in the United States is very high for homeless animals—this fact can be consuming. The biggest con of my job is dealing with the emotion of the business we are in.

There are many, many, many pros of my job. The biggest pro is the people involved in the organization—the ones who make it all happen. It is very rewarding to see the fruits of your labor, and see that what you do can make a difference to animals and for the people of the community. The animals can't really take care of themselves—that's what people are there for—to take care of them. Our business is educating people to better care for their animals. It's rewarding to know you are helping people by providing low-cost spay/neutering, or with adoption, or with education, or helping strengthen the human–animal bond.

Q. What advice would you give to young people who are interested in working in animal shelters?

A. I would tell young people to follow their dreams, and what they are passionate about. The common bond I have found with all the people I have met in this industry is that we all love animals and want to help them. However, it takes a special set of skills to do this.

With a nonprofit organization it is always a matter of doing more with less, especially when it comes to resources. In the past I've seen many people come to this industry after a career in a for-profit. They've already done corporate lives in the rat race, and now they want to give back and get involved in something they feel very passionate about. For young people, they are getting more educated and receive more information through the Internet, so perhaps they may come to this realization (follow your dreams/passions) a lot sooner.

If they are truly dedicated, young people should visit their local animal shelter. However, I must say that because all shelters are separate, young people shouldn't form any initial judgments with only one visit. They should also reach out to other animal welfare organizations, or talk to people already in the industry. I would also encourage them to try and get involved—become a junior volunteer at a shelter is one example of getting experience and earning the community service hours required by many schools.

Q. What is the future employment outlook for your field?

A. Employment opportunities in this field will grow. However, as a professional in the animal welfare industry, my goal is to put the organization out of business. Eventually, there will be no unnecessary euthanasia of adoptable pets—this is everyone's goal. Then these animal shelters could perhaps turn into educational centers to help teach people about the proper care for their animals as well as responsible pet ownership.

Q. Do you find it uplifting to know President Obama decided to adopt from a shelter rather than buy a pedigreed dog?

A. Yes. That is where the education really helped. Even Oprah [Winfrey] adopting from a rescue organization and Ellen DeGeneres adopting her dog—anytime anyone adopts—it all reflects on our work. We are dealing with a pet overpopulation crisis. We are not going to solve this issue by building bigger shelters, it would only be a strategy on how to help deal with it. The root of the problem is really education, and reaching people while they are young to help establish a set of beliefs—ones they can pass on to future generations.

Animal Trainers

OVERVIEW

Animal trainers teach animals to obey commands so the animals can be counted on to perform these tasks in given situations. The animals can be trained for up to several hundred commands, to compete in shows or races, to perform tricks to entertain audiences, to protect property, or to act as guides for the disabled. Animal trainers may work with several types of animals or specialize with one type. Approximately 47,100 animal trainers are employed in the United States.

HISTORY

Animals have been used for their skills for hundreds of years. The St. Bernard has assisted in search-and-rescue missions in the Swiss Alps for more than 300 years. The German shepherd was used in Germany after the First World War to guide blind veterans.

Dorothy Eustis, after visiting the program in Germany, founded the first American program for training guide dogs, called The Seeing Eye, in 1929. Basing the training program on the one that she visited in Potsdam, Eustis's program launched others that were modeled or developed from hers. The Seeing Eye still has one facility in the United States, in Morristown, New Jersey, but dozens of programs now exist for the training of guide dogs for the blind.

Other programs began to utilize the guide dog training system to provide animal-based assistance to other disabled individuals. Most of these

Learn More About It

Hollow, Michele C., and William P. Rives. *The Everything Guide to Working with Animals: From Dog Groomer to Wildlife Rescuer—Tons of Great Jobs for Animal Lovers*. Cincinnati, Ohio: Adams Media Corporation, 2009.

Samansky, Terry S. *Starting Your Career as a Marine Mammal Trainer*. 2d ed. Napa, Calif.: Dolphintrainer.com, 2002.

Sutherland, Amy. *Kicked, Bitten, and Scratched: Life and Lessons at the World's Premier School for Exotic Animal Trainers*. New York: Viking Adult, 2007.

Wilde, Nicole. *So You Want to Be a Dog Trainer*. 2d ed. Santa Clarita, Calif.: Phantom Publishing, 2006.

programs are less than 30 years old, and the majority of the programs were developed in the late 1980s and the 1990s. Programs now exist for a variety of animals over a range of disabilities for which an animal can be of assistance.

Programs to train search-and-rescue dogs in the United States are new, particularly compared to the programs in Europe. The Swiss program inspired search-and-rescue dog training programs in the United States in the 1970s. Various small programs were developed that relied on individuals with specific breeds of dogs to volunteer to train their pets for disaster or search operations. Programs such as the Black Paws for the Newfoundland breed offer certification that is accepted by law enforcement and search teams in selecting animals for search operations. After receiving state-recognized certification, dog and handler teams can choose to continue training for more intensive programs.

The Federal Emergency Management Agency (FEMA) established criteria and certification testing for disaster search dog and handler teams in 1991. Funding from the agency established dog and dog-handler teams that undergo an intensive training program. FEMA-certified teams were used extensively in search-and-recovery operations in the aftermath of the September 11, 2001, terrorist attacks at the Pentagon and World Trade Center.

THE JOB

Many animals are capable of being trained. The techniques used to train them are basically the same, regardless of the type of animal.

An animal trainer (foreground) at Florida's Clearwater Marine Aquarium holds a dolphin as a colleague fits it with a gel sleeve. The dolphin lost her tail after becoming entangled on the line of a crab buoy. A prosthetist devised a tail prosthesis to replace the dolphin's tail. The dolphin's skin is covered by the gel sleeve so the prosthesis does not irritate it. *(Chris O'Meara, AP Photo)*

Animal trainers conduct programs consisting primarily of repetition and reward to teach animals to behave in a particular manner and to do it consistently.

First, trainers evaluate an animal's temperament, ability, and aptitude to determine its trainability. Animals vary in personality, just as people do. Some animals are more stubborn, willful, or easily distracted and would not do well with rigid training programs. All animals can be trained at some level, but certain animals are more receptive to training; these animals are chosen for programs that demand great skill.

One of the most familiar examples is the seeing-eye dog, now usually called a companion animal for the blind. These dogs are trained with several hundred verbal commands to assist their human and to recognize potentially dangerous situations. The dog must be able to, without any command, walk his companion around obstacles on the sidewalk. The companion dog must be able to read streetlights and know to cross at the green, and only after traffic has cleared. The dog must also not be tempted to run to greet other dogs, grab food, or behave as most pet dogs do. Very few dogs make it through the rigorous training program. The successful dogs have proved to be such aids to the visually impaired that similar programs have been developed to train dogs for people who are confined to a wheelchair, or are hearing impaired, or incapable of executing some aspect of a day-to-day routine where a dog can assist.

Animal trainers teach an animal to obey or perform on command or, in certain situations, without command, by painstakingly repeating routines many times and rewarding the animal when it does what is expected. In addition, animal trainers feed, exercise, groom, and generally care for the animals, either handling the duties themselves or supervising other workers. In some training programs, trainers come in and work with the animals; in other programs, such as the companion animal program, the animal lives with the trainer for the duration of the program.

Trainers usually specialize in one type of animal and are identified by this type of animal. *Dog trainers,* for example, may work with police dogs, training them to search for drugs or missing people. The programs to train drug-detecting dogs use different detection responses, but each dog is trained in only one response system. Some dogs are trained to behave passively when the scent is detected, with a quiet signal given to the accompanying police officer that drugs have been detected. The signal can be sitting next to the scent, pointing, or following. Other dogs are trained to dig, tear, and destroy containers that have the drug in them. As one animal trainer from U.S. Customs and Border Protection pointed out, these dogs may be nightmare pets because they can destroy a couch in seconds, but they make great drug-detecting dogs. The common breeds for companion dogs and police dogs are German shepherds, rottweilers, and Labrador retrievers.

Some train guard dogs to protect private property; others train dogs for performance, where the dog may learn numerous stunts or movements with hand commands so that the dog can perform on a stage or in film without the audience hearing the commands spoken from offstage. Shepherding dogs are also trained with whistle or hand commands because commands may have to be given from some distance away from where the dog is working.

Dogs, partly because of the variety of breeds available and partly because of their nature to work for approval, have countless roles for which they are trained. *Pet dog trainers* work with owners to teach their dogs family manners and to help fix destructive or dangerous habits.

Horse trainers specialize in training horses for riding or for harness. They talk to and handle a horse gently to accustom it to human contact, then gradually get it to accept a harness, bridle, saddle, and other riding gear. Trainers teach horses to respond to commands that are either spoken or given by use of the reins and legs. Draft horses are conditioned to draw equipment either alone or as part of a team. Show horses are given special training to qualify them to perform in competitions. Horse trainers sometimes have to retrain animals that have developed bad habits, such as bucking or biting. Besides feeding, exercising, and grooming, these trainers may make arrangements for breeding the horses and help mares deliver their foals.

A highly specialized occupation in the horse-training field is that of *racehorse trainers,* who must create individualized training plans for every horse in their care. By studying the animal's performance record and becoming familiar with its behavior during workouts, trainers can adapt their training methods to take advantage of each animal's peculiarities. Like other animal trainers, racehorse trainers oversee the exercising, grooming, and feeding of their charges. They also clock the running time during workouts to determine when a horse is ready for competitive racing. Racehorse trainers coach jockeys on how best to handle a particular horse during a race and may give owners advice on purchasing horses.

Police horse trainers work with police horses to keep them from startling in crowds or responding to other animals in their presence. As with the police dogs, these animals require a very stable, calm personality that remains no matter what situation the animal works in. Police officers who work with animals on a routine basis develop strong attachments to the animals.

Other animal trainers work with more exotic animals for performance or for health reasons. The dolphins and whales at the Shedd Aquarium in Chicago, for example, are trained by *marine mammal trainers* to roll over, lift fins and tails, and open their mouths on command, so that much veterinary work can be done without anesthesia, which is always dangerous for animals. These skills are demonstrated for the public every day, so they function as a show for people, but the overriding reason for training the dolphins is to keep them healthy. Other training elements include teaching dolphins to retrieve items from the bottom of their pool, so that if any visitor throws or loses something in the pool, divers are not required to invade the dolphins' space.

Animal trainers work with hunting birds, training them to fly after an injury, or to hunt if the bird was found as a hatchling before a parent had trained it. Birds that are successfully trained to fly and hunt can be released into the wild; the others may remain in educational programs where they will perform for audiences. It is, however, illegal to keep any releasable hunting bird for more than one year in the United States.

Each species of animal is trained by using the instincts and reward systems that are appropriate to that species. Hunting birds are rewarded with food; they don't enjoy petting and do not respond warmly to human touch, unless they were hand-raised from hatching by humans. Dogs, on the other hand, respond immediately to petting and gentle handling, unless they were handled inappropriately or viciously by someone. Sea mammals respond to both food and physical contact.

Some animal species are generally difficult to train. Sea otters are extremely destructive naturally and do not train easily. African elephants are much more difficult to train than Asian elephants, and females are much more predictable and trainable than the larger males. Most circus elephants are Asian because they are much easier to handle. Captive elephants, though, kill more handlers and keepers than every other species combined.

REQUIREMENTS

High School

For high school students interested in becoming an animal trainer, courses in anatomy, physiology, biology, and psychology will be helpful. Understanding how the body and mind work helps a trainer understand the best methods for training. Knowledge of psychology will help the trainer recognize behaviors in the animals they train as well as in the people for whom the animals are helping.

Postsecondary Training

Some animal trainer specialties have educational requirements that include a college degree. Animal trainers in circuses and the entertainment field may be required to have some education in animal psychology in addition to their caretaking experience. Zoo and aquarium animal trainers usually must have a bachelor's degree in biology, marine biology, animal science, psychology, or another field related to animal management or animal physiology. Trainers of companion dogs prepare for their work in a three-year course of study at schools that train dogs and instruct the disabled owner-companion.

Most trainers begin their careers as keepers and gain on-the-job experience in evaluating the disposition, intelligence, and "trainability" of the animals they look after. At the same time, they learn to make friends with their charges, develop a rapport with them, and gain their confidence. The caretaking experience is an important building block in the education and success of an animal trainer. Although previous training experience may give job applicants an advantage in being hired, they still will be expected to spend time caring for the animals before advancing to a trainer position.

Establishments that hire trainers often require previous animal-keeping or equestrian experience, as proper care and feeding of animals is an essential part of a trainer's responsibilities. These positions serve as informal apprenticeships. The assistant may get to help an animal trainer on certain tasks but will be able to watch and learn from other tasks being performed around him or her. For example, racehorse trainers often begin as jockeys or grooms in training stables.

Certification or Licensing

Voluntary certification is provided by a variety of organizations, including the Animal Behavior Society, the American College of Veterinary Behaviorists, Certification Council for Professional Dog Trainers, the International Association for the Study of Animal Behavior, the International Association of Animal Behavior Consultants, the International Association of Canine Professionals, and the National Association of Dog Obedience Instructors.

Racehorse trainers must be licensed by the state in which they work. Otherwise, there are no special requirements for this occupation.

Other Requirements

Prospective animal trainers should like and respect animals and have a genuine interest in working with them. With most of the career options for an animal trainer, there is an underlying desire to help people as well. Most trained animals work with people to accomplish a goal, so the relationship between the animal, the trainer, and the owner or companion is an important one. It requires the trainer to be thoughtful, sensitive, and well spoken. Also, the trainer should be prepared to work intensely with an animal and then have that animal go on to work somewhere else. The relationship with the trained animal may not be permanent, so separation is part of the trainer's job.

EXPLORING

Students wishing to enter this field would do well to learn as much as they can about animals, especially animal psychology, either through

Training Helper Dogs

It takes about six months to train guide dogs for the blind. After mastering basic obedience and becoming accustomed to the shoulder harness that is the contact with their owners, the dogs learn to follow basic directions (forward, right, and left), to stop at curbs, to cross streets, and to lead their owners around hazards. The dog trainer also works with the new owners, usually for about a month. Together, they work with the dog and learn to master elevators, revolving doors, subway stations, and trains and buses.

Trainers may also train dogs to work with people who are hearing-impaired or physically disabled. Individualized training programs must be designed for the dogs in order to meet the specific needs of their new owners.

course work or library study. Interviews with animal trainers and tours of their workplaces might be arranged to provide firsthand information about the practical aspects of this occupation.

Volunteering offers an opportunity to begin training with animals and learning firsthand about the tasks and routines involved in managing animals, as well as training them. Part-time or volunteer work in animal shelters, pet-training programs, rescue centers, pet shops, or veterinary offices gives potential trainers a chance to discover whether they have the aptitude for working with animals. Experience can be acquired, too, in summer jobs as animal caretakers at zoos, aquariums, museums that feature live animal shows, amusement parks, and for those with a special interest in horse racing, at stables.

EMPLOYERS

Approximately 47,100 animal trainers are employed in the United States. Animal trainers work for a wide variety of employers, including stables, dog-training and companion pet programs, animal shelters, zoos, aquariums and oceanariums, amusement parks, rescue centers, pet shops, and circuses. Many are self-employed, and a few very successful animal trainers work in the entertainment field, training animal "actors" or working with wild and/or dangerous animals. A number of these positions require a great deal of traveling and even relocating. Although some new zoos and aquariums may open and others may expand their facilities, the number of job opportunities for animal trainers at these facilities will remain relatively small. Companion programs that train animals to assist people who need help in daily living activities will employ an increasing number of trainers.

Tightened security measures around the globe have created demand for bomb-sniffing dogs and their trainers. An increasing number of animal trainers and handlers will be employed by government agencies such as the Federal Aviation Administration and U.S. Customs and Border Protection, Fortune 500 companies, amusement parks, and sports arenas.

STARTING OUT

People who wish to become animal trainers generally start out as animal keepers, stable workers, or caretakers and rise to the position of trainer only after acquiring experience within the ranks of an organization. You can enter the field by applying directly for a job as animal keeper; let your employer or supervisor know about your ambition so you will eventually be considered for promotion. The same applies for volunteer positions. Learning as a volunteer is an excellent way to get hands-on experience, but you should be vocal in your interest in a paid position once you have gotten to know the staff and they have gotten to know you.

You should pay close attention to the training methods of any place at which you are considering working. No reputable organization, regardless of what it trains animals for, should use physical injury to train or discipline an animal. The techniques you learn at your first job determine the position you will qualify for after that. You want to be sure that you are witnessing and learning from an organization that has a sound philosophy and training method for working with animals.

The most coveted positions depend on the animals you want to work with. Sea mammals are a specialty of oceanariums and aquariums, and these positions are fiercely competitive. Dog-training programs are probably the most plentiful and offer the widest range of training philosophies and techniques. There are numerous books on dog training methods that you should consult to know what the differences are.

FEMA works only with established dog and handler teams, who usually work within the emergency systems for the regional or local authorities in some capacity. These teams choose to also be trained within the FEMA guidelines.

ADVANCEMENT

Most establishments have very small staffs of animal trainers, which means that the opportunities for advancement are limited. The progression is from animal keeper to animal trainer. A trainer who directs or supervises others may be designated head animal trainer or senior animal trainer.

Some animal trainers go into business for themselves and, if successful, hire other trainers to work for them. Others become agents for animal acts. But promotion may mean moving from one organization to another and may require relocating to another city, depending on what animal you specialize in.

EARNINGS

Salaries of animal trainers can vary widely according to specialty and place of employment. Salaries ranged from less than $16,920 to $52,130 a year or more in 2009, according to the U.S. Department of Labor (DOL). The median salary for animal trainers was $26,930. Those who earn higher salaries are in upper management and spend more time running the business than working with animals.

In the field of racehorse training, however, trainers are paid an average fee of $35 to $50 a day for each horse, plus 10 percent of any money their horses win in races. Depending on the horse and the races it runs, this can exceed the average high-end earnings for a trainer. Show horse trainers may earn as much as $30,000 to $35,000 a year. Trainers in business for themselves set their own fees for teaching both horses and owners.

Benefits for full-time workers include vacation and sick time, health, and sometimes dental, insurance, and pension or 401(k) plans. Self-employed trainers must provide their own benefits. Approximately 54 percent of animal trainers are self-employed.

WORK ENVIRONMENT

The working hours for animal trainers vary considerably, depending on the type of animal, performance schedule, and whether travel is involved. For some trainers, such as those who work with show horses, educational programs with hunting birds, or new animals being brought into zoos and aquariums, the hours can be long and quite irregular. Travel is common and will probably include responsibility for seeing to the animals' needs while on the road. This can include feeding, creative housing, and driving with the animal. For one program director of a rescue center that works with injured hawks, it means traveling frequently for educational shows with a suitcase full of frozen rats and chicks for food.

Much of the work is conducted outdoors. In winter, trainers may work indoors, but depending on the animal, they may continue outdoor training year-round. If the animal is expected to work or perform outdoors in winter, it has to be trained in winter as well. Companion animals have to cope with every type of weather, so the trainer is responsible for training and testing the animal accordingly.

Working with certain animals requires physical strength; for example, it takes arm strength to hold a falcon on your wrist for an hour, or to control an 80-pound dog that does not want to heel. Other aspects of the work may require lifting, bending, or extended periods of standing or swimming. Trainers of aquatic mammals, such as dolphins and seals, work in water and must feel comfortable in aquatic environments.

Patience is essential to the job as well. Just as people do, animals have bad days where they won't work well and respond to commands. So even the best trainer encounters days of frustration where nothing seems to go well. Trainers must spend long hours repeating routines and rewarding their pupils for performing well, while never getting angry with them or punishing them when they fail to do what is expected. Trainers must be able to exhibit the authority to keep animals under control without raising their voices or using physical force. Calmness under stress is particularly important when dealing with wild animals.

OUTLOOK

This field is expected to grow much faster than the average for all careers through 2018, according to the DOL. Although criticism of animals used for purely entertainment purposes has reduced the number used for shows and performances, programs have expanded for companion animals and animals used in work settings. Also, a growing number of animal owners are seeking training services for their pets.

An increased number of trainers will be needed to train the growing number of search-and-rescue and bomb-sniffing dog teams. The latter will be in demand to ensure the safety of airports, government buildings, corporations, amusement parks, sports facilities, and public utilities.

In all fields, applicants must be well qualified to overcome the heavy competition for available jobs. Competition for jobs will be especially strong for marine mammal trainers and horse trainers. Some openings may be created as zoos and aquariums expand or provide more animal shows in an effort to increase revenue.

FOR MORE INFORMATION

Visit the association's Web site for dog training tips; career, education, and certification information; and to read a sample issue of ADPT Chronicle of the Dog.

Association of Pet Dog Trainers (ADPT)
101 North Main Street, Suite 610
Greenville, SC 29601-4841
Tel: 800-738-3647
E-mail: information@apdt.com
http://www.apdt.com

For general information about zoos, aquariums, oceanariums, and wildlife parks, contact

Association of Zoos and Aquariums
8403 Colesville Road, Suite 710
Silver Spring, MD 20910-3314
Tel: 301-562-0777
http://www.aza.org

Canine Companions for Independence is a nonprofit organization that assists people with disabilities by providing trained assistance dogs and ongoing support.

Canine Companions for Independence
PO Box 446
Santa Rosa, CA 95402-0446
Tel: 800-572-2275
http://www.cci.org

Contact the council for information on certification for dog trainers.

Certification Council for Professional Dog Trainers
Professional Testing Corporation
1350 Broadway, 17th Floor
New York, NY 10018-7702
Tel: 212-356-0682
E-mail: administrator@ccpdt.org
http://www.ccpdt.org

The Delta Society currently provides certification programs in animal evaluation and in training animal handlers for animal-assisted therapy and companion animal training.

Delta Society
875 124th Avenue NE, Suite 101
Bellevue, WA 98055-2531

Tel: 425-679-5500
E-mail: info@deltasociety.org
http://www.deltasociety.org

This organization rescues and trains dogs to help people live better and more productive lives.
Dogs for the Deaf
10175 Wheeler Road
Central Point, OR 97502-9360
Tel: 541-826-9220
E-mail: info@dogsforthedeaf.org
http://www.dogsforthedeaf.org

Visit the association's Web site for information on careers, endangered species, useful books and other publications, and student membership (for "anyone who is interested in the objectives of the association, and supports them").
International Marine Animal Trainers' Association
1200 South Lake Shore Drive
Chicago, IL 60605-2490
Tel: 312-692-3193
E-mail: info@imata.org
http://www.imata.org

Visit the association's Web site for information on entering the field, schools, and publications.
National Association of Dog Obedience Instructors
PO Box 1439
Socorro, NM 87801-1439
Tel: 505-890-5957
http://www.nadoi.org

This is a professional membership association for pet boarders, sitters, groomers, animal trainers, and pet suppliers. It offers a membership category for any "individual who is interested in the pet care industry, but who does not presently operate a non-veterinary pet care business." Visit the association's Web site for information on training opportunities, membership, networking events, and pet health.
Pet Care Services Association
401 North Michigan Avenue, Suite 2200
Chicago, IL 60611-4245
Tel: 800-218-9123
http://www.petcareservices.org

Aquarists

QUICK FACTS

School Subjects
Biology
Earth science

Personal Skills
Following instructions
Technical/scientific

Work Environment
Indoors and outdoors
One location with some
  travel

Minimum Education Level
Bachelor's degree

Salary Range
$15,590 to $23,000 to
$40,000

Certification or Licensing
Required

Outlook
Little or no change

DOT
412

GOE
03.02.01

NOC
6483

O*NET-SOC
39-2021.00

OVERVIEW

Aquarists (pronounced, like "aquarium," with the accent on the second syllable) work for aquariums, oceanariums, and marine research institutes. They maintain aquatic exhibits. Among other duties, they feed the fish, check water quality, clean the tanks, and collect and transport new specimens.

HISTORY

In 1853, the world's first public aquarium opened in Regents Park in London. Similar public aquariums opened throughout England, France, and Germany over the next 15 years. Many of the early aquariums closed because the fish could not survive in the conditions provided. By the early 1870s, knowledge of aeration, filtering, and water temperature had increased, and new aquariums opened.

In 1856, the U.S. government established what is today the Division of Fishes of the Smithsonian Institution's National Museum of Natural History. Over the next 50 years interest in fish and their environments grew rapidly. The Scripps Institution of Oceanography was established in 1903, and the Woods Hole Oceanographic Institute was established in 1930.

Today's notable aquariums include the John G. Shedd Aquarium, Chicago; the National Aquarium, Baltimore; the Georgia Aquarium, Atlanta; the New York Aquarium, New York City; the Steinhart Aquarium, San Francisco; and the Audubon Aquarium of the Americas, New Orleans. Many aquariums recreate diverse aquatic environments, such as coral reefs, river bottoms, or various coastlines, in large tanks.

Aquariums on the Web

Alaska SeaLife Center (Seward)
http://www.alaskasealife.org

Aquarium of the Bay (San Francisco, Calif.)
http://www.aquariumofthebay.org

Audubon Aquarium of the Americas (New Orleans)
http://www.auduboninstitute.org/visit/aquarium

Georgia Aquarium (Atlanta)
http://www.georgiaaquarium.org

John G. Shedd Aquarium (Chicago)
http://www.sheddaquarium.org

Miami Seaquarium (Miami, Fla.)
http://www.miamiseaquarium.com

Monterey Bay Aquarium (Monterey, Calif.)
http://www.montereybayaquarium.org

Mystic Aquarium and Institute for Exploration (Mystic, Conn.)
http://www.mysticaquarium.org

National Aquarium Baltimore
http://www.aqua.org

New England Aquarium (Boston)
http://www.neaq.org

New York Aquarium (New York City)
http://www.nyaquarium.com

Oregon Coast Aquarium (Newport)
http://www.aquarium.org

Seattle Aquarium (Seattle, Wash.)
http://www.seattleaquarium.org

Steinhart Aquarium (San Francisco)
http://www.calacademy.org/academy/exhibits/aquarium

Waikiki Aquarium (Waikiki, Hawaii)
http://www.waquarium.org

Some aquariums also have oceanariums—huge tanks that allow visitors to view marine animals from above as well as from the sides. Popular oceanariums include those at the Miami Seaquarium in Miami, Florida, and the Monterey Bay Aquarium in Monterey, California.

THE JOB

Aquarists work for aquariums, oceanariums, and marine research institutes. Aquarists are not animal trainers and do not work on marine shows. They do, however, support the staff who do. Their work is generally technical and requires a strong science background. With increased experience and education, aquarists may, in time, become involved in research efforts at their institution or become promoted to higher professional positions such as curator.

Aquarists' job duties are similar to those of zookeepers. Aquarists feed fish and other marine animals, maintain exhibits, and conduct research. They work on breeding, conservation, and educational programs.

Aquarists clean and take care of tanks every day. They make sure pumps are working, check water temperatures, clean glass, and sift sand. Some exhibits have to be scrubbed by hand. Aquarists also change the water and vacuum tanks routinely. They water plants in marsh or pond exhibits.

Food preparation and feeding are important tasks for aquarists. Some animals eat live food and others eat cut-up food mixtures. Some animals need special diets prepared and may have to be individually fed.

Aquarists carefully observe all the animals in their care. They must understand their normal habits (including mating, feeding, sleeping, and moving) in order to be able to judge when something is wrong. Aquarists write daily reports and keep detailed records of animal behavior.

Many aquarists are in charge of collecting and stocking plants and animals for exhibits. They may have to make several trips a year to gather live specimens.

REQUIREMENTS

High School

If you want to become an aquarist, get your start in high school. Take as many science classes as you can; biology and zoology are especially important. Learn to pay attention to detail; marine science involves a good deal of careful record keeping.

Postsecondary Training

Most aquariums, along with other institutions that hire aquarists, require that an applicant have a bachelor's degree in biological sciences, preferably with course work in such areas as parasitology (the study of parasites and their hosts), ichthyology (the study of fishes), or other aquatic sciences. As the care of captive animals becomes a more complex discipline, it's no longer enough to apply without a four-year degree.

Certification or Licensing

Aquarists must be able to dive, in both contained water, to feed fish and maintain tanks, and in open water, on trips to collect new specimens. You'll need to have scuba certification, with a rescue diver classification, for this job. Organizations such as PADI provide basic certification. Potential employers will expect you to be able to pass a diving physical examination before taking you on as an aquarist. You may also need to have a special collector's permit from the state in which you work that allows you to gather samples for your aquarium.

Other Requirements

As an aquarist, you may be required to travel at different times throughout the year, to participate in research expeditions and collecting trips. On a more basic level, aquarists need to be in good physical shape, with good hearing and visual acuity. Some employers also require a certain strength level—say, the ability to regularly exert 100 pounds of force—since equipment, feed, and the animals themselves can be heavy and often unwieldy. Good communication and teamwork skills are also important.

EXPLORING

In addition to formal education, many aquariums, like other types of museums, look for a strong interest in the field before hiring an applicant. Most often, they look for a history of volunteering. That means you need to look for every avenue you can find to work around fish or other animals. Do as much as your schedule allows. Even working part time or volunteering at a local pet store counts. Also, be sure to ask your career guidance counselor for information on marine science careers and opportunities for summer internships or college scholarships offered by larger institutes.

You should also consider joining the Association of Zoos and Aquariums (AZA), which offers an associate membership category "for zoo and aquarium professionals, as well as other interested parties, who want to support and forward the mission, vision, and goals of AZA."

EMPLOYERS

Aquarists most often work in zoos, public aquariums, or in research jobs with marine science institutes.

STARTING OUT

Full-time jobs for aquarists can be scarce, especially for those just starting in the field. Part-time or volunteer positions with zoos, aquariums, science institutes, nature centers, or even pet stores could provide valuable preliminary experience that may eventually lead to a full-time position.

ADVANCEMENT

The usual career path for an aquarist progresses from intern/volunteer through part-time work to full-fledged aquarist, senior aquarist, supervisor, and finally, curator. Each step along the path requires additional experience and often additional education. Curators generally are expected to have a Ph.D. in a relevant marine science discipline, for example. The career path of an aquarist depends on how much hands-on work they like to do with animals. Other options are available for aquarists who are looking for a less "down and dirty" experience.

EARNINGS

Aquariums often are nonprofit institutions, limiting the earnings ability in this job somewhat. In general, aquarists make between $23,000 and $40,000 a year. Salaries for nonfarm animal caretakers (a career category that includes aquarists) ranged from less than $15,590 to $31,660 or more in 2009, according to the U.S. Department of Labor.

Aquariums offer fairly extensive benefits, including health insurance, 401(k) plans, continuing education opportunities, tuition reimbursement, and reciprocal benefits with many other cultural institutions.

WORK ENVIRONMENT

Aquarists may work indoors or outdoors, depending on the facility for which they work and the exhibit to which they're assigned. Aquarists spend a lot of time in the water. Their day will be filled with a variety of tasks, some repetitive, like feeding, others unusual, such as working with rescued marine mammals, perhaps. In the beginning, aquarists work under the supervision of a senior aquarist or supervisor and may work as part of a team. Aquarists also can expect to travel as part of the job.

OUTLOOK

There is, in general, little change in the availability of positions for aquarists. While terrestrial zoos have begun to add aquarium complexes to their campuses in growing numbers, an actual boom in the construction of new aquariums is unlikely at this time. Many aquarists do advance to other positions, however, so openings do become available. Aquarists with advanced degrees and training who are willing to relocate will have the best employment opportunities.

FOR MORE INFORMATION

Visit the alliance's Web site for information on marine mammals, internships, and publications.
Alliance of Marine Mammal Parks and Aquariums
E-mail: ammpa@aol.com
http://www.ammpa.org

Visit the AAZK Web site to read the online publication Zoo Keeping as a Career *(which includes information about the career of aquarist).*
American Association of Zoo Keepers (AAZK)
3601 29th Street, SW, Suite 133
Topeka, KS 66614-2054
Tel: 785-273-9149
http://aazk.org

For information on membership, a list of accredited zoos throughout the world, and careers in aquatic and marine science, including job listings, contact
Association of Zoos and Aquariums
8403 Colesville Road, Suite 710
Silver Spring, MD 20910-3314

Tel: 301-562-0777
http://www.aza.org

For information on diving instruction and certification, contact
PADI
30151 Tomas Street
Rancho Santa Margarita, CA 92688-2125
Tel: 800-729-7234
http://www.padi.com/scuba

Equestrian Management Workers

OVERVIEW

Equestrian management workers include a wide variety of positions, such as *farriers, horse breeders, horse trainers, judges, jockeys, stable managers, riding instructors, farm managers, racetrack managers, equine insurance adjusters, breed association managers, race association managers,* and related business, sales, and marketing positions. According to the American Horse Council, there are more than 1.4 million people employed in the horse management industry.

HISTORY

Historically valued for work and transportation, horses have been in use since 2000 B.C., when they were domesticated in Babylonia (present-day Iraq). Evidence indicates that horses were in use in Egypt three hundred years later. Chariots with mounted soldiers were popular in parades, and equestrian displays were featured in early Olympic Games in Greece and at ancient Roman celebrations. By the 14th century, horses were used by knights, with a fast, light horse (a palfrey) used for travel, and a sturdier war-horse (like a quarterhorse) used to carry the knight in battle. Because of the extreme weight of the knight's and the horse's armor, the horses had to be durable, stocky animals.

Pages were young boys, usually born to noble families, who learned under the tutelage of knights and

QUICK FACTS

School Subjects
Agriculture
Biology
Business

Personal Skills
Following instructions
Technical/scientific

Work Environment
Indoors and outdoors
One location with some
  travel

Minimum Education Level
Varies by position

Salary Range
$15,000 to $30,000 to
  $65,000+

Certification or Licensing
Required for certain specialties

Outlook
About as fast as the average

DOT
410

GOE
03.02.01

NOC
8253

O*NET-SOC
39-2011.00, 45-2021.00,
  45-2093.00

squires how to care for and ride horses, and acquired the other skills they were expected to know. As they improved and got older, they would serve as a knight's squire, learning the skills for battle, and assisting the knight in actual battles. Squires worked with the knight's horses and led the war-horse as the knight rode the palfrey. He then kept the palfrey safe while the knight fought or jousted. Eventually a squire might become a knight himself.

The swiftest transportation across land for the next five hundred years was by horse. Horses were either ridden or used to pull carriages or other transport. Roads were unreliable, unpassable in winter or rainy weather, and travelers had to find places to stay that could accommodate horses as well. The expense of buying and keeping a horse, or a team of horses for some carriages, restricted their use to wealthy families. Mules were more common for transporting goods, and people frequently traveled by walking, even for journeys of hundreds or thousands of miles. Travelers on foot could go eight to 12 miles a day on average, so it took at least twice as long on foot as it did by horse to travel.

In the 16th century, Spanish conquistadors brought the first horses to America. The horse population increased as horses were left to breed in wild packs. Eventually Native American tribes incorporated horses into their lives, capturing and domesticating the animals. European settlers also were familiar with horses for both transportation and farming purposes, so they also brought and used horses.

Interest in horses changed from functional to recreational uses in the late 1800s and early 1900s. Trains replaced horse travel as the fastest transportation across land. Trains were not only faster, they were more reliable and safer for travelers. Gasoline- and diesel-powered vehicles such as the car and the tractor replaced the horse for both local travel and farming needs. By the 1930s, in all but the least developed countries, the horse became an animal for leisure activities only. Horses are used now for Western and English riding, rodeos, and horse racing, and rarely for other activities. Stable owners and landowners hire the workers who care for the horses used in these activities.

THE JOB

Horses are owned, ridden, raced, and shown in every state in the nation. With nearly 7 million domesticated horses in the United States alone, the staff needed to care for and train these animals is immense. From riding trainers to the people who manage stables

Caring for a Horse

Horses need extensive care to remain healthy. Some of the necessary activities to maintain a horse's health are the following:

- Vaccinations for influenza and tetanus with annual booster shots

- Deworming, with regular feeding of deworming chemicals, and isolation of newly arrived horses to avoid spreading worms

- Grooming to maintain a horse's cleanliness and good condition; grooming massages a horse, promoting good circulation and preventing disease

- Good housing, with stabling during cold periods, especially for fine coated horses; the best form of stabling allows the horse room to move around and lie down

- Fresh water, in a stream or container

- Access to pasture, with approximately 1.5 acres for every horse, and safe and adequate fencing

- Adequate nutrition, based on the type of horse and the time of year

with dozens of animals, the range of jobs and the range of places to work is large.

Equestrian management positions include "contact" and "noncontact" positions. Contact jobs are hands-on positions actually working with horses, at a track, on a farm, or with a breeding association. Noncontact jobs may involve working in the marketing department of a racetrack, as a breeder, in a riding stable, or as a salesperson for equipment, feed, insurance, or equine pharmaceuticals.

Equine-related careers require long hours, whether a person is working directly with horses or in an office setting. Regardless of the position, employers look for people with a knowledge of horses, flexibility, and a willingness to start small and work their way up. For example, a *riding instructor* may work from 6:00 A.M. to 10:00 P.M. if a schedule mandates such lesson times. There may be long breaks, but during show season, days can be long. An instructor may take two or 20 pupils to a horse show and be responsible for coaching them before, during, and after classes. Riding instructors may work with students who are looking to enter a riding competition or who are just riding for pleasure. Students range from youngsters to retired people looking to develop a new hobby.

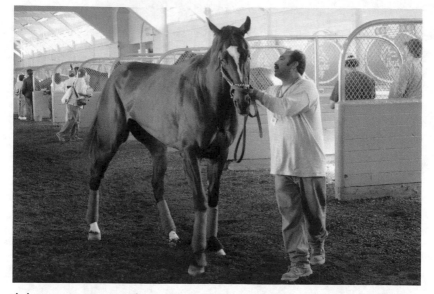

A horse groom steadies prize-winning horse Zenyatta in the paddock during "schooling" for an upcoming race. *(Reed Saxon, AP Photo)*

Training can be for dressage, which involves riding a horse through a series of complex maneuvers to demonstrate the agility and responsiveness of the horse and the control of the rider. Jumping is riding the horse through a varied obstacle course. Combined training, or eventing, is the triathlon of equestrian sports, incorporating dressage, cross-country jumping, and show jumping. Riders compete at all levels of competition, including Olympic levels. Trainers usually specialize, unless they train for eventing.

A *stable manager* is similar to a store manager. Responsibilities include ensuring feed and bedding are well stocked and ordered, as well as medicating and monitoring sick or injured horses. The duties of stable managers include hiring personnel to clean stalls and feed, exercise, and groom horses. In a small operation, the manager may do such tasks. He or she may organize clinics or shows at a stable for large groups of riders, and work with judges, stewards, food vendors, and various horse organizations. Turning a horse out to a paddock or pasture daily is usually necessary for a horse's health. In a large stable, a manager must know the personality, temperament, and physical needs of each horse. The types of things the manager notes about each horse can be which horses get along with certain riders or other horses, which ones must be left alone in a paddock, which have physical ailments, and such details as when the horse was last ridden, groomed, inspected, fed, watered, and checked by the vet. New horses have to be introduced to the herd by a process of increasing interaction spent with a new horse and its pasture mates.

Horse grooms care for and maintain racehorses. They feed, bathe, and brush the horses each day. They also are responsible for cleaning the horses' stalls on a regular basis.

Jockeys ride racehorses. A *harness driver* sits in a sulky and guides trotters around the track; a *steeplechase jockey* rides a horse cross-country on a course with large brush jumps; and a *flat racing jockey* rides horses on a flat track at varying distances. Many jockeys work as freelancers, riding for different barns, trainers, and owners. A good jockey may be hired by a specific barn for a whole season because of a particularly good relationship with a certain horse. Generally, jockeys have fairly stable working hours during racing season but usually begin early in the morning and finish in early evening after a day of racing.

Judges are used at all levels and disciplines with the horse industry. Horse showing is popular from the 4-H club level to the international show circuit. Judges grade and place riders by their excellence. Some judges travel internationally, and others may officiate each summer at a local show.

Veterinary technicians are the equivalent of nurses in the veterinary field. They tend to general animal care and do tests, administer medicine, perform radiology exams or ultrasound therapy, and provide wound care.

Farriers, a word that comes from the medieval French word for iron (ferrour), refers to people who shoe horses and care for their hooves and feet. Horses' hooves grow the way fingernails do, so they require trimming and grooming, and, to protect the hoof, a farrier may put an iron ring on the bottom of the hoof. These are the semicircle items called horseshoes. A farrier may have to make horseshoes, but he or she must always customize the shoe for each horse, even if the iron rings are not made by hand.

The equine industry is a business like any other, so capable administrators with a knowledge of horses and office management are necessary. One administrative position is that of an *equine marketing representative,* whose duties include promoting and organizing horse shows and races. Marketing representatives also develop brochures and videos of horses and their offspring to promote various breed associations. They may work in insurance, providing life insurance coverage for valuable horses used for breeding, performing, or racing.

REQUIREMENTS

For information on requirements specific to the careers of animal breeders and technicians and veterinary technicians, see those articles.

High School

High school students should take biology courses. If your school has any riding classes, clubs, or teams, you should consider participating. Any experience around horses is helpful and gives you an item for your resume.

Postsecondary Training

College courses for equestrian management workers can include anatomy, animal physiology, health, and business management. Each will give you some flexibility in job training.

Riding instructors or trainers must have an extensive background in riding or teaching and possibly a certificate from an accredited school.

Stable management positions may also require a degree from an accredited two-year program. Students learn everything from feeding rations and veterinary maintenance to handling troublesome horses and managing a show. Long hours may be required depending upon how busy the stable is with lessons and how many horses are in the facility.

Farriers must earn a certificate from an accredited school (usually a six-week full-time course), and an apprenticeship with an experienced farrier is highly recommended.

A college degree is not mandatory for sales positions, but it is preferable.

Some colleges and universities offer equine management or science programs, and students often take business administration courses. Visit http://horseschools.com for a list of equestrian management programs.

Certification or Licensing

The American Riding Instructors Association offers certification to riding instructors who pass a written and oral test. They must also submit a video/DVD that shows their work as an instructor.

Depending on the show and riding discipline, some judges may need accreditation or training experience or must attend certain courses and clinics.

For dressage competitions, certification may be required. The U.S. Dressage Federation (USDF) provides certification in four categories: certified instructor/trainer; training through second level;

recognized teacher; training through second level; certified instructor/trainer; third through fourth level; and recognized teacher; third through fourth level.

Other Requirements

Riding instructors must have patience and the ability to calm nervous students.

Being a judge requires good horsemanship, a good eye, and several years' experience in the horse industry.

To become a trainer, a person must know how to groom and care for horses and build a reputation as a competent trainer who is sensitive to a horse's needs and abilities.

Being a farrier requires great physical strength, especially in the arms and back. It is not absolutely necessary to have a background with horses; however, a good and respected farrier will have an excellent eye in spotting problems with a horse's gait and the ability to know what is wrong with its movements just from watching.

Knowledge of the horse industry and enthusiasm are required to be a successful sales representative.

Computer skills are increasingly important in this field. Anyone expecting to advance through management ranks should have a college degree.

EXPLORING

Visiting a local stable, taking riding lessons, and joining 4-H are the easiest ways to begin to explore the career possibilities in equestrian management. Any experience with horses will only help your career. Access to most of the jobs described here can be gained by starting at the bottom and working with and around horses. A part-time job at a stable or grooming horses for a trainer will net valuable experience for the potential jockey, trainer, or salesperson.

EMPLOYERS

More than 1.4 million people are employed in the horse management industry. Equestrian management workers are employed at farms, veterinarian offices, animal hospitals, breeding associations, race tracks, riding stables and schools, manufacturers, and sales organizations.

STARTING OUT

Aside from administrators and managers, anyone interested in a career with horses should take riding lessons. Some stables need part-time and full-time help depending on the season and location. Many larger facilities offer positions where a person may clean stalls, feed and groom horses, and maintain stables. It is possible to negotiate an exchange of services for riding lessons, where you can gain experience both as a rider as well as a groom, in a volunteer position. Job opportunities can also be found on the Internet at http://www.equistaff.com.

Although all states have stables and riding schools, Kentucky is the heart of the horse industry, with many other southern states dominating the market with their internationally acclaimed breeders and stables. Texas and California also have a large percentage of the horse populations in every category, from racing horses to work horses.

ADVANCEMENT

It is possible to go from lower level grooming jobs to higher level positions. A farrier or veterinary technician may become self-employed after building a reputation and customer base.

With proper certification and a four-year college degree, it's possible to start work in entry-level management and progress. Top management positions require a business degree.

EARNINGS

Equistaff.com reports the following average salaries for equestrian management workers by specialty in 2010: trainers, $39,912; riding instructors, $29,708; veterinary assistants, $26,371; and grooms/stablehands, $22,043.

Grooms and stablehands earn from $7.25 an hour (minimum wage) to $11 an hour. Some receive extras like free riding lessons, a percentage of purse or prize money, or paid training or certification fees. Approximately 20 percent receive free housing and utilities. Riding instructors earn an average of $40 per hour for individual lessons and $25 per hour for group lessons. Show horse riders earn $20 per hour on average. Racehorse exercise riders earn $10 per head for riding 1/2 hour or less. About one-third of the largest racing and training facilities offer insurance benefits and other perks to their exercise riders. Managers and trainers earned from $10.01 to $26.04 per hour. They may receive such benefits as free housing, medical insurance, bonuses, a vehicle, or free board for their own horses.

The yearly earnings of stable managers and other administrators vary depending on the size and success of the farm, but in general are somewhere between $20,000 and $65,000 or more. Horse breeders may earn from $19,000 to $50,000 a year. Horse trainers earn from $15,000 to $55,000 a year depending on years of experience, reputation, commissions on horses they have sold, and on the breeds. If a trainer can rent out all of his stalls, instead of putting his own horses in them, he can earn more money to pay for expenses.

Most judges have other jobs and get paid for each show they judge. Their pay ranges from $300 to $500 per show.

Farriers may earn $18,000 a year to start, and the earning ceiling for most farriers is about $30,000 a year. However, an experienced and well-sought-after farrier who charges $100 to $200 per horse and can shoe seven to nine horses a day can earn much more.

Marketing representatives start at $18,000 in entry-level positions, but over several years their earning potential is unlimited. Sales representatives start low at $15,000 a year, but usually also receive bonuses or commissions. Their income potential, like the marketing representative, is limited only by the market and their own drive.

Benefits for full-time workers include vacation and sick time, health, and sometimes dental, insurance, and pension or 401(k) plans. Self-employed workers must provide their own benefits.

WORK ENVIRONMENT

Most positions in the horse industry require long hours, especially during show season. Many contract, or farm, positions are seasonal, requiring employees to have some other form of employment to support their equine career. Persons interested in these careers should enjoy working with horses in the entire spectrum of conditions.

OUTLOOK

The horse industry has been on the decline in recent years. The recession, revised tax laws, and competition with other sports and forms of gambling have taken dollars away from the industry.

Many farms have consolidated, but opportunities for farriers and veterinary technicians are plentiful. A lot of farm work is seasonal, and most people who work with horses have another form of income they use to support their horse business.

Still, the demand for all types of breeds of horses will continue, particularly for recreation and showing. It is estimated that there are 9.2 million horses in the United States, which generate more than 1.4 million full-time equivalent jobs.

FOR MORE INFORMATION

For information on equestrian careers, contact the following organizations:

American Horse Council
1616 H Street NW, 7th Floor
Washington, DC 20006-4918
Tel: 202-296-4031
E-mail: ahc@horsecouncil.org
http://www.horsecouncil.org

United States Equestrian Federation
4047 Iron Works Parkway
Lexington, KY 40511-8516
Tel: 859-258-2472
http://www.usef.org

For information on certification, contact
American Riding Instructors Association
28801 Trenton Court
Bonita Springs, FL 34134-3337
Tel: 239-948-3232
E-mail: riding-instructor@comcast.net
http://www.riding-instructor.com

For information on programs and awards, contact
American Youth Horse Council
577 North Boyero Avenue
Pueblo West, CO 81007-1001
Tel: 719-594-9778
E-mail: info@ayhc.com
http://www.ayhc.com

For industry information, contact
Thoroughbred Owners and Breeders Association
PO Box 910668
Lexington, KY 40591-0668
Tel: 859-276-2291
E-mail: toba@toba.org
http://www.toba.org

For information on equestrian competitions, contact
United States Eventing Association
525 Old Waterford Road, NW

Leesburg, VA 20176-2050
Tel: 703-779-0440
E-mail: info@useventing.com
http://www.useventing.com

For industry information, contact
U.S. Dressage Federation
4051 Iron Works Parkway
Lexington, KY 40511-8483
Tel: 859-971-2277
http://www.usdf.org

Farmers

QUICK FACTS

School Subjects
Agriculture
Business

Personal Skills
Leadership/management
Mechanical/manipulative

Work Environment
Primarily outdoors
Primarily multiple locations

Minimum Education Level
High school diploma

Salary Range
$18,900 to $32,350 to
$103,210+

Certification or Licensing
Voluntary

Outlook
Decline

DOT
421

GOE
03.01.01

NOC
8251

O*NET-SOC
11-9011.00, 11-9011.02,
11-9012.00, 45-1011.00

OVERVIEW

Farmers either own or lease land on which they raise crops, such as corn, wheat, tobacco, cotton, vegetables, or fruits; raise animals or poultry; or maintain herds of dairy cattle for the production of milk. Whereas some farmers may combine several of these activities, most specialize in one specific area. They are assisted by *farm laborers*—either hired workers or members of farm families—who perform various tasks. There are approximately 985,900 plant and animal farmers and ranchers employed in the United States. This article will focus solely on farmers who raise farm animals.

HISTORY

In colonial America, almost 95 percent of the population were farmers, planting such crops as corn, wheat, flax, and, further south, tobacco. Livestock including hogs, cattle, sheep, and goats were imported from Europe. Farmers raised hay to feed livestock and often just enough other crops to supply their families with a balanced diet throughout the year. Progress in science and technology in the 18th and 19th centuries allowed for societies to develop in different directions, and to build other industries, but over one-half of the world's population is still engaged in farming today.

In the early 20th century, farmers raised a variety of crops along with cattle, poultry, and dairy cows. Farm labor was handled by the farmers and their families. Farmers were very self-sufficient, living on their farms and maintaining their own equipment and storage. Between 1910 and 1960, when horsepower was replaced by

A farmer feeds his calves. *(Jeff Greenberg, The Image Works)*

mechanized equipment, about 90 million acres previously devoted to growing hay for the feeding of horses could be planted with other crops. Advances in farming techniques and production led to larger farms and more specialization by farmers. Farmers began to focus on growing one or two crops. About this time, more tenant farmers entered the business, renting land for cash or share of the crops.

Farmers doubled their output between 1950 and 1980, but there were fewer of them. In that time, the farm population decreased from 23 million to 6 million. After 1980, many farmers began supplementing their household income with off-farm jobs and businesses.

Today, some small-scale farmers are finding success by catering to niche markets such as organic foods and specialty crops. Others are even branching off into aquaculture—the commercial farming of fish.

THE JOB

Farmers who raise and breed animals for milk or meat are called *livestock* and *cattle farmers*. There are various types of farmers that fall into this category.

Livestock farmers generally buy calves from ranchers who breed and raise them. They feed and fatten young cattle and often raise their own corn and hay to lower feeding costs. They need to be familiar with cattle diseases and proper methods of feeding. They provide their cattle with fenced pasturage and adequate shelter from rough weather. Some livestock farmers specialize in breeding stock for sale to ranchers and dairy farmers. These specialists maintain and improve purebred animals of a particular breed. Bulls and cows are then sold to ranchers and dairy farmers who want to improve their herds.

Sheep ranchers raise sheep primarily for their wool. Large herds are maintained on rangeland in the western states. Since large areas of land are needed, the sheep rancher must usually buy grazing rights on government-owned lands.

Although *dairy farmers'* first concern is the production of high-grade milk, they also raise corn and grain to provide feed for their animals. Dairy farmers must be able to repair the many kinds of equipment essential to their business and know about diseases, sanitation, and methods of improving the quantity and quality of the milk.

Dairy animals must be milked twice every day, once in the morning and once at night. Records are kept of each cow's production of milk to ascertain which cows are profitable and which should be traded or sold for meat. After milking, when the cows are at pasture, the farmer cleans the stalls and barn by washing, sweeping, and sterilizing milking equipment with boiling water. This is extremely important because dairy cows easily contract diseases from unsanitary conditions, and this in turn may contaminate the milk. Dairy farmers must have their herds certified to be free of disease by the U.S. Department of Health and Human Services.

The great majority of *poultry farmers* do not hatch their own chicks but buy them from commercial hatcheries. The chicks are kept in brooder houses until they are seven or eight weeks old and are then transferred to open pens or shelters. After six months, the hens begin to lay eggs, and roosters are culled from the flock to be sold for meat.

The primary duty of poultry farmers is to keep their flocks healthy. They provide shelter from the chickens' natural enemies and from extreme weather conditions. The shelters are kept extremely clean, because diseases can spread through a flock rapidly. The poultry farmer selects the food that best allows each chicken to grow or produce to its greatest potential while at the same time keeping costs down.

Raising chickens to be sold as broilers or fryers requires equipment to house them until they are six to 13 weeks old. Farmers specializing in the production of eggs gather eggs at least twice a day and more often in very warm weather. The eggs then are stored in a cool place, inspected, graded, and packed for market. The poultry farmer who specializes in producing broilers is usually not an independent producer but is under contract with a backer, who is often the operator of a slaughterhouse or the manufacturer of poultry feeds.

Aquaculture farmers, also known as *aquaculturists, fish farmers, fish culturists,* and *mariculturists,* raise fish, shellfish, or other aquatic life (such as aquatic plants) under controlled conditions for profit and/or human consumption.

Beekeepers set up and manage beehives and harvest and sell the excess honey that bees don't use as their own food. The sale of honey is less profitable than the business of cultivating bees for lease to farmers to help pollinate their crops.

In addition to the different types of farmers, there are two different types of farming management careers: the *farm operator* and the *farm manager.*

The farm operator either owns his or her own farm or leases land from other farms. Farm operators' responsibilities vary depending on the type of farm they run, but in general they are responsible for making managerial decisions. They determine the best time to seed, fertilize, cultivate, spray, and harvest. They keep extensive financial and inventory records of the farm operations, which are now done with the help of computer programs.

Farm operators perform tasks ranging from caring for livestock to erecting sheds. The size of the farm often determines what tasks the operators handle themselves. On very large farms, operators hire employees to perform tasks that operators on small farms would do themselves.

The farm manager has a wide range of duties. The owner of a large livestock farm may hire a farm manager to oversee a single activity, such as feeding the livestock. In other cases, a farm manager may oversee the entire operation of a small farm for an absentee owner. Farm management firms often employ highly skilled farm managers to manage specific operations on a small farm or to oversee tenant farm operations on several farms.

Farmers and farm managers make a wide range of administrative decisions. In addition to their knowledge of animal science, they determine how to market the foods they produce. They keep an eye on the commodities markets to see which crops are most profitable. They take out loans to buy farm equipment or additional land for cultivation. They keep up with new methods of production and new markets. Farms today are large, complex businesses, complete with the requisite anxiety over cash flow, competition, markets, and production.

REQUIREMENTS

High School

Take classes in math, accounting, and business to prepare for the management responsibilities of running a farm. To further assist you in management and the use of farming-related technology, take computer classes. Chemistry, biology, and earth science classes can help you understand the various processes of agricultural production. Technical and shop courses will help you to better understand agricultural machinery. With county extension courses, you can keep abreast of developments in farm technology.

Postsecondary Training

Although there are no specific educational requirements for this field, every successful farmer, whether working with crops or animals, must know the principles of soil preparation and cultivation, disease control, and machinery maintenance, as well as a mastery of business practices and bookkeeping. Livestock and dairy farmers should enjoy working with animals and have some background in animal science, breeding, and care.

The state land-grant universities across the country (with at least one in every state) were established to encourage agricultural research and to educate young people in the latest advancements in farming. They offer agricultural programs that award bachelor's degrees as well as shorter programs in specific areas. Many students earn a degree in business with a concentration in agriculture, agricultural economics and business, animal science, agronomy, crop and fruit science, dairy science, farm management, or horticulture. Some universities offer advanced studies in horticulture, animal science, agronomy, and agricultural economics. Most students in agricultural colleges are also required to take courses in farm management, business, finance, and economics. Two-year colleges often have programs leading to associate's degrees in agriculture. It is highly recommended that farm managers and farmers earn at least an associate's degree in agriculture or a related subject (or business with a concentration in agriculture) in order to stay up-to-date with technological advancements and changes in farming practices.

A bachelor's degree in aquaculture or fish and wildlife biology are the primary paths into the field of aquaculture. A minor in business or accounting may also be valuable to a prospective aquaculturist. Course work focuses on hydrology, fisheries biology, fish culture, and hatchery management and maintenance.

Many people become beekeepers by receiving informal on-the-job training working with an experienced beekeeper. Community or junior colleges that offer agriculture classes may also provide another avenue for learning about honey production and bee care. Finally, some states may offer apprenticeship programs in beekeeping.

Certification or Licensing

The American Society of Farm Managers and Rural Appraisers offers farm operators voluntary certification as an accredited farm manager. Certification requires five years' experience working on a farm, an academic background—a bachelor's or preferably a master's degree in a branch of agricultural science—and completion of courses covering the business, financial, and legal aspects of farm management.

Other Requirements

You'll need to keep up-to-date on livestock- and poultry-raising methods throughout the world. You must be flexible and innovative enough to adapt to new technologies that will raise livestock more efficiently. You should also have good mechanical aptitude and be able to work with a wide variety of tools and machinery. Other important traits include a good work ethic, determination, organizational skills, and business acumen.

EXPLORING

Most people who become farmers have grown up on farms; if your family doesn't own a farm there are opportunities for part-time work as a hired hand, especially during seasonal operations.

In addition, organizations such as the National 4-H Council (http://4-h.org) and the National FFA Organization (https://www. ffa.org) offer good opportunities for learning about, visiting, and participating in farming activities. Agricultural colleges often have their own farms where students can gain actual experience in farm operations in addition to classroom work.

EMPLOYERS

Approximately 985,900 plant and animal farmers and ranchers are employed in the United States. Nearly 80 percent of farmers are self-employed, working on land they've inherited, purchased, or leased. Those who don't own land, but who have farming experience, may find work on large commercial farms or with agricultural supply companies as consultants or managers. They may also own other businesses, such as those that specialize in farm equipment sales and service.

STARTING OUT

Livestock farmers generally start by renting property and sometimes animals on a share-of-the-profits basis with the owner. Government lands can be rented for pasture as well. Later, when the livestock farmer wants to own property, it is possible to borrow based on the estimated value of the leased land, buildings, and animals. Dairy farmers can begin in much the same way. However, loans are becoming more difficult to obtain. After several years of lenient loan policies, financial institutions in farm regions have tightened their requirements.

ADVANCEMENT

Farmers advance by buying their own farms or additional acreage to increase production and income. With a farm's success, a farmer can also invest in better equipment and technology and can hire managers and workers to attend to much of the farm's operation. In farming, as in other fields, a person's success depends greatly on education, motivation, and keeping up with the latest developments.

EARNINGS

Farmers' incomes vary greatly from year to year, since the prices of farm products fluctuate according to weather conditions and the amount and quality of what all farmers were able to produce. A farm that shows a large profit one year may show a loss for the following year. Most farmers, especially those running small farms, earn incomes from nonfarm activities that are several times larger than their farm incomes. Farm incomes also vary greatly depending on the size and type of farm.

The Economic Research Service of the U.S. Department of Agriculture reports that the average farm household income was $76,258 in 2009. This income, it is important to note, includes earnings from off-farm jobs, businesses, and other sources.

Farmers and ranchers earned a median annual salary of $32,350 in 2009, according to the U.S. Department of Labor (DOL). Salaries ranged from less than $18,900 to more than $91,710.

Farm managers who worked full time had median annual earnings of $59,450 in 2009, according to the DOL. The lowest paid 10 percent of farm managers earned less than $31,680 a year, and the top paid 10 percent of all farm managers earned $103,210 or more a year.

Farmers must provide their own benefits, such as health and life insurance and a savings and pension program. Farm managers and operators typically receive benefits from their employer.

WORK ENVIRONMENT

The farmer's daily life has its rewards and dangers. Machine-related injuries, exposure to the weather, and illnesses caused by allergies or animal-related diseases are just some of the hazards that farmers face on a regular basis. In addition, farms are often isolated, away from many conveniences and necessities, such as immediate medical attention.

Farming can be a difficult and frustrating career, but for many it is a satisfying way of life. The hours are long and the work is physically strenuous, but working outdoors and watching the fruits of one's labor grow before one's eyes can be very rewarding. The changing seasons bring variety to the day-to-day work. Farmers seldom work five eight-hour days a week. Dairy farmers and other livestock farmers work seven days a week year round.

OUTLOOK

Employment of farmers and ranchers is expected to decline through 2018, according to the DOL. The department predicts that employment for farm and ranch managers will grow more slowly than the average for all careers (which, in DOL terminology, means that there will actually be some employment growth) during that same time span as owners of farm property seek managers to oversee land and agricultural workers. Every year can be different for farmers, as production, expansion, and markets are affected by weather, exports, and other factors. Land prices are expected to drop some, but so are the prices for grain, hogs, and cattle. Throughout the 20th century, the U.S. government actively aided farmers, but in recent years has attempted to step back from agricultural production.

Large corporate farms are fast replacing the small farmer, who is being forced out of the industry by the spiraling costs of feed, grain, chemicals, land, and equipment. The late 1970s and early 1980s were an especially hard time for farmers. Many small farmers were forced to give up farming; some lost farms that had been in their families for generations. Some small-scale farmers, however, have found opportunities in organic food production, farmers' markets, and similar market niches that require more direct personal contact with their customers.

Despite the great difficulty in becoming a farmer today, there are many agriculture-related careers that involve people with farm production, marketing, management, and agribusiness. Those with an interest in farming will likely have to pursue these alternative career paths.

FOR MORE INFORMATION

The American Beekeeping Federation acts on behalf of the bee-keeping industry on issues affecting the interests and the economic viability of the various sectors of the industry. The organization offers a free beginning beekeeping information packet and sponsors an essay contest in conjunction with 4-H. For more information, contact

American Beekeeping Federation
3525 Piedmont Road, Building 5, Suite 300
Atlanta, GA 30305-1578
Tel: 404-760-2875
E-mail: info@abfnet.org
http://www.abfnet.org

The AFBF Web site features legislative news, state farm bureau news, online brochures, and information on Farm Bureau Programs such as AFBF Young Farmers & Ranchers Program. This program, for ages 18 to 35, offers educational conferences, networking opportunities, and competitive events.

American Farm Bureau Federation (AFBF)
600 Maryland Avenue, SW, Suite 1000W
Washington, DC 20024-2520
Tel: 202-406-3600
http://www.fb.org

For information on certification, contact

American Society of Farm Managers and Rural Appraisers
950 South Cherry Street, Suite 508
Denver, CO 80246-2664
Tel: 303-758-3513
http://www.asfmra.org

To learn about farmer-owner cooperatives and how cooperative businesses operate, contact
National Council of Farmer Cooperatives
50 F Street, NW, Suite 900
Washington, DC 20001-1530
Tel: 202-626-8700
http://www.ncfc.org

For information on farm policies, homeland security issues, and other news relating to the agricultural industry, visit the USDA Web site.
U.S. Department of Agriculture (USDA)
1400 Independence Avenue, SW
Washington, DC 20250-0002
Tel: 202-720-2791
http://www.usda.gov

For information about aquaculture, contact
World Aquaculture Society
143 J. M. Parker Coliseum
Louisiana State University
Baton Rouge, LA 70803-0001
Tel: 225-578-3137
https://www.was.org

Marine Biologists

QUICK FACTS

School Subjects
Biology
Earth science

Personal Skills
Mechanical/manipulative
Technical/scientific

Work Environment
Indoors and outdoors
Primarily multiple locations

Minimum Education Level
Bachelor's degree

Salary Range
$33,254 to $44,176 to
$155,020+

Certification or Licensing
Required for certain
positions

Outlook
About as fast as the average

DOT
041

GOE
02.03.03

NOC
2121

O*NET-SOC
19-1020.01, 25-1042.00

OVERVIEW

Marine biologists study species of plants and animals living in saltwater, their interactions with one another, and how they influence and are influenced by environmental factors. Marine biology is a branch of the biological sciences, and biologists in this area work in myriad industries, including government agencies, universities, aquariums, and fish hatcheries, to name a few. They generally work either in a laboratory setting or in the field, which in this case means being in or on the ocean or its margins.

HISTORY

Marine biologists started to make their study into a real science around the 19th century with a series of British expeditions. In 1872, the HMS *Challenger* set sail with scientists Sir Charles Wyville Thomson and Sir John Murray on the most important oceanographic mission of all time. Over four years, they traveled 69,000 miles and cataloged 4,717 new species of marine plants and animals. Many marine scientists view the reports from this expedition as the basis of modern oceanography.

Before this time, marine scientists believed that sea creatures inhabited only shallow waters. They believed that the intense cold, pressure, and darkness below about 1,800 feet could not support life. Then, in the late 1860s, the HMS *Lightning* and the HMS *Porcupine* made hauls from below 14,400 feet that contained bizarre new creatures.

Scientists began to build precision equipment for measuring oceanic conditions. Among these were thermometers that could gauge

Learn More About It

Cramer, Deborah. *Smithsonian Ocean: Our Water, Our World.*
Washington, D.C.: Smithsonian, 2008.
DeGalan, Julie. *Great Jobs for Environmental Studies Majors.* 2d
ed. New York: McGraw-Hill, 2008.
Heitzmann, Ray. *Opportunities in Marine Science and Maritime
Careers.* Rev. ed. New York: McGraw-Hill, 2006.
Kaplan, Eugene H. *Sensuous Seas: Tales of a Marine Biologist.*
Princeton, N.J.: Princeton University Press, 2006.
Stephens, Lester D., and Dale R. Calder. *Seafaring Scientist: Alfred
Goldsborough Mayor, Pioneer in Marine Biology.* Columbia,
S.C.: University of South Carolina Press, 2006.

the temperature at any depth, containers that could be closed at a
desired depth to collect seawater, and coring instruments used to
sample bottom sediments. Scientists also figured out techniques for
measuring levels of salt, oxygen, and nutrients right on board ship.

Twentieth-century innovations such as underwater cameras, oxygen tanks, submersible craft, and heavy-duty diving gear that can
withstand extremes of cold and pressure have made it possible for
marine biologists to observe sea creatures in their natural habitats.

THE JOB

Marine biologists study and work with sea creatures in their natural
environment, the oceans of the world and tidal pools along shore-
lines, as well as in laboratories. These scientists are interested in
knowing how the ocean's changing conditions, such as temperature and chemical pollutants, can affect the plants and animals that
live there. For example, what happens when certain species become
extinct or are no longer safe to be eaten? Marine biologists can begin
to understand how the world's food supply is diminished and help
come up with solutions that can change such problem situations.

The work of these scientists is also important for improving
and controlling sport and commercial fishing. Through underwater exploration, marine biologists have discovered that humans
are damaging the world's coral reefs. They have also charted the
migration of whales and counted the decreasing numbers of certain
species. They have observed dolphins being accidentally caught
in tuna fishermen's nets. By writing reports and research papers

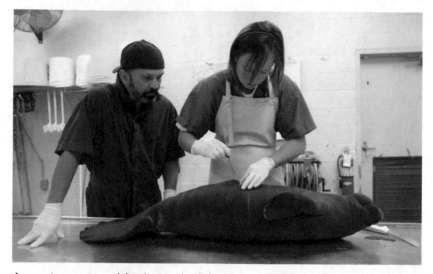

A marine mammal biologist (right) at the Manatee Mammal Pathology Lab and a visiting biologist begin a necropsy on a manatee calf. The calf is believed to have died from exposure to below-normal temperatures. *(Chris O'Meara, AP Photo)*

about such discoveries, a marine biologist can inform others about problems that need attention and begin to make important changes that could help the world.

To study plants and animals, marine biologists spend some of their work time in the ocean wearing wetsuits to keep warm (because of the frigid temperature below the surface of the sea) and scuba gear to breathe underwater. They gather specimens with a slurp gun, which sucks fish into a specimen bag without injuring them. They must learn how to conduct their research without damaging the marine environment, which is delicate. Marine biologists must also face the threat to their own safety from dangerous fish and underwater conditions.

Marine biologists also study life in tidal pools along the shoreline. They might collect specimens at the same time of day for days at a time. They would keep samples from different pools separate and keep records of the pool's location and the types and measurements of the specimens taken. This ensures that the studies are as accurate as possible. After collecting specimens, they keep them in a portable aquarium tank on board ship. After returning to land, which may not be for weeks or months, marine biologists study specimens in a laboratory, often with other scientists working on the same study.

They might, for example, check the amount of oxygen in a sea turtle's bloodstream to learn how the turtles can stay underwater for so long, or measure elements in the blood of an arctic fish to discover how it can survive frigid temperatures.

One growing subspecialty is marine biotechnology. *Marine biotechnologists* study ocean organisms that may be used for biotechnological applications, including drug development or nontoxic coatings that repel fouling organisms (such as zebra mussels) on intake pipes in power plants.

REQUIREMENTS

High School

If you are interested in this career, begin your preparations by taking plenty of high school science classes, such as biology, chemistry, and earth science. Also take math classes and computer science classes, both of which will give you skills that you will use in doing research. In addition, take English classes, which will also help you develop research skills as well as writing skills. And, because you will probably need to extend your education beyond the level of a bachelor's degree, consider taking a foreign language. Many graduate programs require their students to meet a foreign language requirement.

Postsecondary Training

In college, take basic science courses such as biology, botany, and chemistry. However, your class choices don't end there. For instance, in biology you might be required to choose from marine invertebrate biology, ecology, oceanography, genetics, animal physiology, plant physiology, and aquatic plant biology. You might also be required to choose several more specific classes from such choices as ichthyology, vertebrate structure, population biology, developmental biology, biology of microorganisms, evolution, and cell biology. Classes in other subjects will also be required, such as computer science, math (including algebra, trigonometry, calculus, analytical geometry, and statistics), and physics.

Although it is possible to get a job as a marine biologist with just a bachelor's degree, such jobs likely will be low-paying technician positions with little advancement opportunities. Some positions in the field are available with a master's degree, but most marine biologists have a doctoral degree. Students at the graduate level begin to develop an area of specialization, such as aquatic chemical ecology (the study of chemicals and their effect on aquatic environments) and bioinformatics (the use of computer science, math, and statistics to analyze genetic information). Master's degree programs generally take two to three years to complete. Programs leading to a Ph.D. typically take four to five years to complete.

Certification or Licensing

If you are going to be diving, organizations like PADI provide basic certification. Training for scientific diving is more in-depth and requires passing an exam. It is also critical that divers learn cardiopulmonary resuscitation (CPR) and first aid. Also, if you'll be handling hazardous materials such as formaldehyde, strong acids, or radioactive nucleotides, you must be licensed.

Other Requirements

You should have an ability to ask questions and solve problems, observe small details carefully, do research, and analyze mathematical information. You should be inquisitive and must be able to think for yourself. This is essential to the scientific method. You must use your creative ability and be inventive in order to design experiments; these are the scientist's means of asking questions of the natural world. Working in the field often requires some strength and physical endurance, particularly if you are scuba diving or if you are doing fieldwork in tidepools, which can involve hiking over miles of shore at low tide, keeping your footing on weedy rocks, and lifting and turning stones to find specimens.

EXPLORING

Explore this career and your interest in it by joining your high school's science club. If the club is involved in any type of projects or experiments, you will have the opportunity to begin learning to work with others on a team as well as develop your science and lab skills. If you are lucky enough to live in a city with an aquarium, be sure to get either paid or volunteer work there. This is an excellent way to learn about marine life and about the life of a marine biologist. Visit Sea Grant's Marine Careers Web site (http://www.marine careers.net) for links to information on internships, volunteerships, and other activities, such as sea camps.

You can begin diving training while you are in high school. If you are between the ages of 10 and 14, you can earn a junior open water diver certification from PADI. When you turn 15 you can upgrade your certification to open water diver.

EMPLOYERS

Employers in this field range from pharmaceutical companies researching marine sources for medicines to federal agencies that regulate marine fisheries, such as the National Oceanographic and Atmospheric Administration's Fisheries Service. Aquariums hire marine biologists to collect and study specimens.

After acquiring many years of experience, marine biologists with Ph.D.'s may be eligible for faculty positions at academic and research institutions such as the Scripps Institution of Oceanography or the University of Washington's School of Oceanography.

Marine products companies that manufacture carrageenan and agar (extracted from algae and used as thickening agents in foods) hire marine biologists to design and carry out research.

Jobs in marine biology are based mostly in coastal areas, though some biologists work inland as university professors or perhaps as paleontologists who search for and study marine fossils.

STARTING OUT

With a bachelor's degree only, you may be able to get a job as a laboratory technician in a state or federal agency. Some aquariums will hire you straight out of college, but generally it's easier to get a paid position if you have worked as a volunteer at an aquarium. You will need a more advanced degree to get into more technical positions such as consulting, writing for scientific journals, and conducting research.

Web sites are good resources for employment information. If you can find the human resources section of an aquarium's home page, it will tell you whom to contact to find out about openings and may even provide job listings. Federal agencies may also have Web sites with human resource information.

Professors who know you as a student might be able to help you locate a position through their contacts in the professional world.

Another good way to make contacts is by attending conferences or seminars sponsored by aquatic science organizations such as the American Society of Limnology and Oceanography or the Mid-Atlantic Marine Education Association.

ADVANCEMENT

Lab technicians with four-year degrees may advance to become senior lab techs after years with the same lab. Generally, though, taking on greater responsibility or getting into more technical work means having more education. Those wanting to do research (in any setting) will need a graduate degree or at least be working on one. To get an administrative position with a marine products company or a faculty position at a university, marine biologists need at least a master's degree, and those wanting to become senior scientists at a marine station or full professors must have a doctoral degree.

EARNINGS

Salaries vary quite a lot depending on factors such as the person's level of education, the type of work (research, teaching, etc.), the size, location, and type of employer (for example, large university, government agency, or private company), and the person's level of work experience. According to the National Association of Colleges and Employers, those seeking their first job and holding bachelor's degrees in biological and life sciences had average salary offers of $33,254 in July 2009. The American Society of Limnology and Oceanography reports that those with bachelor's degrees may start out working for federal government agencies at the pay grades GS-5 to GS-7. In 2010, yearly earnings at the GS-5 level ranged from $27,431 to $35,657, and yearly earnings at the GS-7 level ranged from $33,979 to $44,176. College biological science teachers (including those who specialize in marine biology) had median annual salaries of $73,980 in 2009, according to the U.S. Department of Labor. Salaries ranged from less than $41,060 to more than $155,020. Marine biologists who hold top-ranking positions and have much experience, such as senior research scientists, may make more than these amounts.

Benefits vary by employer but often include such extras as health insurance and retirement plans.

WORK ENVIRONMENT

Most marine biologists don't actually spend a lot of time diving. However, researchers might spend a couple of hours periodically breathing from a scuba tank below some waters, like Monterey Bay or the Gulf of Maine. They might gather samples from the deck of a large research vessel during a two-month expedition, or they might meet with several other research biologists.

In most marine biology work, some portion of time is spent in the lab, analyzing samples of seawater or collating data on a computer. Many hours are spent in solitude, reading papers in scientific journals or writing papers for publication.

Instructors or professors work in classrooms interacting with students and directing student lab work.

Those who work for an aquarium, as consultants for private corporations, or in universities work an average of 40 to 50 hours a week.

OUTLOOK

There are more marine biologists than there are top positions at present. Changes in the earth's environment, such as global climate change and increased levels of heavy metals in the global water cycle, will most likely prompt more research and result in slightly more jobs in different subfields. Education is extremely important in this field. Most marine biologists in basic research positions have a Ph.D. Those with just a bachelor's or master's degree often work as science or engineering technicians, high school biology teachers, and in nonscientist positions related to biology such as marketing, sales, publishing, and research management.

Greater need for smart management of the world's fisheries, research by pharmaceutical companies into deriving medicines from marine organisms, and cultivation of marine food alternatives such as seaweeds and plankton are other factors that may increase the demand for marine biologists in the near future. Because of strong competition for jobs, however, employment should grow about as fast as the average for all careers.

FOR MORE INFORMATION

This organization for diving scientists stresses diving safety and offers internships for college students.
American Academy of Underwater Scientists
Dauphin Island Sea Lab
101 Bienville Boulevard
Dauphin Island, AL 36528-4603
Tel: 251-861-7504
E-mail: aaus@disl.org
http://www.aaus.org

For information on fisheries science, contact
American Fisheries Society
5410 Grosvenor Lane
Bethesda, MD 20814-2144
Tel: 301-897-8616
http://www.fisheries.org

The Education section of the institute's Web site has information on a number of careers in biology.
American Institute of Biological Sciences
1444 I Street, NW, Suite 200
Washington, DC 20005-6535
Tel: 202-628-1500
http://www.aibs.org

Visit the ASLO Web site for information on careers, education, and publications, contact
American Society of Limnology and Oceanography (ASLO)
5400 Bosque Boulevard, Suite 680
Waco, TX 76710-4446
Tel: 800-929-2756
E-mail: business@aslo.org
http://www.aslo.org

Contact this society for ocean news and information on membership.
The Oceanography Society
PO Box 1931
Rockville, MD 20849-1931
Tel: 301-251-7708
E-mail: info@tos.org
http://www.tos.org

For information on diving instruction and certification, contact
PADI
30151 Tomas Street
Rancho Santa Margarita, CA 92688-2125
Tel: 800-729-7234
http://www.padi.com/scuba

This center for research and education in global science currently runs more than 300 research programs and uses a fleet of four ships to conduct expeditions over the entire globe. For more information, contact
Scripps Institution of Oceanography
University of California-San Diego
8602 La Jolla Shores Drive
La Jolla, CA 92037-1508
Tel: 858-534-3624
E-mail: scrippsnews@ucsd.edu
http://www-sio.ucsd.edu

The society seeks to save wildlife and wild lands. Visit its Web site to learn more about programs for teens and to read sample articles from Wildlife Conservation Magazine.

Wildlife Conservation Society
2300 Southern Boulevard
Bronx, NY 10460-1068
Tel: 718-220-5100
http://www.wcs.org

The Wildlife Society offers Careers in Wildlife Conservation, *which details more than 10 careers in the field. The publication is available at its Web site, along with information on other publications, student chapters, certification, and membership for college students or anyone who is interested in wildlife conservation and management.*

The Wildlife Society
5410 Grosvenor Lane, Suite 200
Bethesda, MD 20814-2144
Tel: 301-897-9770
E-mail: TWS@wildlife.org
http://joomla.wildlife.org

For links to career information and sea programs, visit the following Web sites:

Careers in Oceanography, Marine Science, and Marine Biology
http://ocean.peterbrueggeman.com/career.html

Sea Grant Marine Careers
http://www.marinecareers.net

For reference lists, links to marine labs, summer intern and course opportunities, and links to career information, check out the following Web site:

Marine Biology Web
http://life.bio.sunysb.edu/marinebio/mbweb.html

Naturalists

QUICK FACTS

School Subjects
Biology
Earth science
English

Personal Skills
Communication/ideas
Technical/scientific

Work Environment
Primarily outdoors
One location with some
travel

Minimum Education Level
Bachelor's degree

Salary Range
$20,000 to $45,000 to
$75,000+

Certification or Licensing
None available

Outlook
About as fast as the average

DOT
049

GOE
12.01.01

NOC
2121

O*NET-SOC
19-1031.03

OVERVIEW

The primary role of *naturalists* is to educate the public about the environment and maintain the natural environment on land specifically dedicated to wilderness populations. Their primary responsibilities are preserving, restoring, maintaining, and protecting a natural habitat. Among the related responsibilities in these jobs are teaching, public speaking, writing, giving scientific and ecological demonstrations, and handling public relations and administrative tasks. Naturalists may work in a variety of environments, including private nature centers; local, state, and national parks and forests; wildlife museums; and independent nonprofit conservation and restoration associations. Some of the many job titles a naturalist might hold are *wildlife manager, fish and game warden, fish and wildlife officer, land steward, wildlife biologist*, and *environmental interpreter. Natural resource managers, wildlife conservationists*, and *ecologists* sometimes perform the work of naturalists.

HISTORY

Prior to the 17th century, there was little support for environmental preservation. Instead, wilderness was commonly seen as a vast resource to be controlled. This view began to change during the early years of the Industrial Revolution, when new energy resources were utilized, establishing an increasing need for petroleum, coal, natural gas, wood, and water for hydropowered energy. In England and France, for example, the rapid depletion of forests caused by the increased use of timber for powering the new industries led to demands for forest conservation.

The United States, especially during the 19th century, saw many of its great forests razed, huge tracts of land leveled for open-pit mining and quarrying, and increased disease with the rise of air pollution from the smokestacks of factories, home chimneys, and engine exhaust. Much of the land damage occurred at the same time as a dramatic depletion of wildlife, including elk, antelope, deer, bison, and other animals of the Great Plains. Some types of bear, cougar, and wolf became extinct, as did several kinds of birds, such as the passenger pigeon. In the latter half of the 19th century, the U.S. government set up a commission to develop scientific management of fisheries, established the first national park (Yellowstone National Park in Wyoming, Idaho, and Montana), and set aside the first forest reserves. The modern conservation movement grew out of these early steps.

States also established parks and forests for wilderness conservation. Parks and forests became places where people, especially urban dwellers, could acquaint themselves with the natural settings of their ancestors. Naturalists, employed by the government, institutions of higher education, and various private concerns, were involved not only in preserving and exploring the natural reserves but also in educating the public about the remaining wilderness.

Controversy over the proper role of U.S. parks and forests began soon after their creation (and continues to this day), as the value of these natural areas for logging, recreation, and other human activities conflicted with the ecological need for preservation. President Theodore Roosevelt, a strong supporter of the conservation movement, believed nevertheless in limited industrial projects, such as dams, within the wilderness areas. Despite the controversy, the system of national parks and forests expanded throughout the 20th century. Today, the Agriculture and Interior Departments, and, to a lesser extent, the Department of Defense, have conservation responsibilities for soil, forests, grasslands, water, wildlife, and federally owned land.

In the 1960s and early 1970s, the hazards posed by pollution to both humans and the environment highlighted the importance of nature preservation and public education. Federal agencies were established, such as the Environmental Protection Agency, the Council on Environmental Quality, and the National Oceanic and Atmospheric Administration. Crucial legislation was passed, including the Wilderness Act (1964) and the Endangered Species Act (1969). Naturalists have been closely involved with these conservation efforts and others, shouldering the responsibility to communicate to the public the importance of maintaining diverse ecosystems and to help restore or balance ecosystems under threat.

THE JOB

Because of the impact of human populations on the environment, virtually no area in the United States (except Alaska) is truly wild. Land and the animal populations require human intervention to help battle against the human encroachment that is damaging or hindering wildlife. Naturalists work to help wildlife maintain or improve their hold in the world.

The work can be directly involved in maintaining individual populations of animals or plants, overseeing whole ecosystems, or promoting the work of those who are directly involved in the maintenance of the ecosystem. *Fish and wildlife officers* (or *fish and game wardens*) work to preserve and restore the animal populations, including migratory birds that may only be part of the environment temporarily. *Wildlife managers* and *range conservationists* oversee the combination of plants and animals in their territories.

Fish and wildlife officers and wardens study, assist, and help regulate the populations of fish, hunted animals, and protected animals throughout the United States. They may work directly in the parks and reserves, or they may oversee a region within a particular state, even if there are no parklands there. Fish and game wardens control the hunting and fishing of wild populations to make sure that the populations are not overharvested during a season. They monitor the populations of each species off season as well as make sure the species is thriving but is not overpopulating and running the risk of starvation or territory damage. Most people hear about the fish and game wardens when a population of animals has overgrown its territory and needs either to be culled (selectively hunted) or moved. Usually this occurs with the deer population, but it can also apply to predator animals such as the coyote or fox, or scavenger animals such as the raccoon. Because the practice of culling animal populations arouses controversy, the local press usually gives wide coverage to such situations.

The other common time to hear about wildlife wardens is when poaching is uncovered locally. Poaching can be hunting or fishing an animal out of season or hunting or fishing a protected animal. Although we think of poachers in the African plains hunting lions and elephants, poaching is common in the United States for animals such as mountain lions, brown bears, eagles, and wolves. Game wardens target and arrest poachers; punishment can include prison sentences and steep fines.

Wildlife managers, *range managers,* and *conservationists* work to maintain the plant and animal life in a given area. Wildlife managers can work in small local parks or enormous national parks. Range managers work on ranges that have a combination of domestic livestock and wild population. The U.S. government has leased and permitted farmers to graze and raise livestock on federally held ranges, although this program is under increasing attack by environmentalists. Range managers must ensure that both the domestic and wild populations are living side by side successfully. They make sure that the population of predatory wild animals does not increase enough to deplete the livestock and that the livestock does not overgraze the land and eliminate essential food for the wild animals. Range managers and conservationists must test soil and water for nutrients and pollution, count plant and animal populations in every season, and keep in contact with farmers using the land for reports of attacks on livestock or the presence of disease.

Wildlife managers also balance the needs of the humans using or traveling through the land they supervise and the animals that live in or travel through that same land. They keep track of the populations of animals and plants and provide food and water when it is lacking naturally. This may involve airdrops of hay and grain during winter months to deer, moose, or elk populations in remote reaches of a national forest, or digging and filling a water reservoir for animals during a drought.

Naturalists in all these positions often have administrative duties such as supervising staff members and volunteers, raising funds (particularly for independent nonprofit organizations), writing grant applications, taking and keeping records and statistics, and maintaining public relations. They may write articles for local or national publications to inform and educate the public about their location or a specific project. They may be interviewed by journalists for reports concerning their site or their work.

Nature walks are often given to groups as a way of educating people about the land and the work that goes into revitalizing and maintaining it. Tourists, schoolchildren, amateur conservationists and naturalists, social clubs, and retirees commonly attend these walks. On a nature walk, the naturalist may point out specific plants and animals, identify rocks, and discuss soil composition or the natural history of the area (including special environmental strengths and problems). The naturalist may even discuss the indigenous people of the area, especially in terms of how they adapted to the unique aspects of their particular environment. Because such a variety of topics may be brought up, the naturalist must be an environmental generalist, familiar with such subjects as biology, botany, geology, geography, meteorology, anthropology, and history.

Demonstrations, exhibits, and classes are ways that the naturalist can educate the public about the environment. For example, to help children understand oil spills, the naturalist may set up a simple demonstration showing that oil and water do not mix. Sometimes the natural setting already provides an exhibit for the naturalist. Dead fish, birds, and other animals found in a park may help demonstrate the natural life cycle and the process of decomposition. Instruction may also be given on outdoor activities, such as hiking and camping.

For some naturalists, preparing educational materials is a large part of their job. Brochures, fact sheets, pamphlets, and newsletters may be written for people visiting the park or nature center. Materials might also be sent to area residents in an effort to gain public support.

One aspect of protecting any natural area involves communicating facts and debunking myths about how to respect the area and the flora and fauna that inhabit it. Another aspect involves tending managed areas to promote a diversity of plants and animals. This may mean introducing trails and footpaths that provide easy yet noninvasive access for the public; it may mean cordoning off an area to prevent foot traffic from ruining a patch of rare moss; or it may mean instigating a letter-writing campaign to drum up support for legislation to protect a specific area, plant, or animal. It may be easy to get support for protecting the snowshoe rabbit; it is harder to make the public understand the need to preserve and maintain a batcave.

Some naturalists, such as *directors of nature centers or conservation organizations,* have massive administrative responsibilities. They might recruit volunteers and supervise staff, organize long- and short-term program goals, and handle record keeping and the budget. To raise money, naturalists may need to speak publicly on a regular basis, write grant proposals, and organize and attend scheduled fund-raising activities and community meetings. Naturalists also try to increase public awareness and support by writing press releases and organizing public workshops, conferences, seminars, meetings, and hearings. In general, naturalists must be available as resources for educating and advising the community.

REQUIREMENTS

High School
If you are interested in this field, you should take a number of basic science courses, including biology, chemistry, and earth science.

Botany courses and clubs are helpful, since they provide direct experience monitoring plant growth and health. Animal care experience, usually obtained through volunteer work, also is helpful. Take English courses in high school to improve your writing skills, which you will use when writing grant proposals and conducting research.

Postsecondary Training

An undergraduate degree in environmental, physical, or natural sciences is generally the minimum educational requirement for becoming a naturalist. Common college majors are biology, forestry, wildlife management, natural resource and park management, natural resources, botany, zoology, chemistry, natural history, and environmental science. Course work in economics, history, anthropology, English, international studies, and communication arts are also helpful.

Graduate education is increasingly required for employment as a naturalist, particularly for upper level positions. A master's degree in natural science or natural resources is the minimum requirement for supervisory or administrative roles in many of the nonprofit agencies, and several positions require either a doctorate or several years of experience in the field. For positions in agencies with international sites, work abroad is necessary and can be obtained through volunteer positions such as those with the Peace Corps or in paid positions assisting in site administration and management.

Other Requirements

If you are considering a career in this field, you should like working outdoors, as most naturalists spend the majority of their time outside in all kinds of weather. However, along with the desire to work in and with the natural world, you need to be capable of communicating with the human world as well. Excellent writing skills are helpful in preparing educational materials and grant proposals.

Seemingly unrelated skills in this field, such as engine repair and basic carpentry, can be essential to managing a post. Because of the remote locations of many of the work sites, self-sufficiency in operating and maintaining the equipment allows the staff to lose fewer days because of equipment breakdown.

EXPLORING

One of the best ways to learn about the job of a naturalist is to volunteer at one of the many national and state parks or nature centers. These institutions often recruit volunteers for outdoor work. College students, for example, are sometimes hired to work as summer or part-time nature guides. Outdoor recreation and training organizations, such as Outward Bound (http://www.outwardbound.org) and the National Outdoor Leadership School (http://www.nols.edu), are especially good resources. Most volunteer positions, though, require a high school diploma and some college credit.

You should also consider college internship programs. In addition, conservation programs and organizations throughout the country and the world offer opportunities for volunteer work in a wide variety of areas, including working with the public, giving lectures and guided tours, and working with others to build or maintain an ecosystem. For more frequent, up-to-date information, you can read newsletters, such as *Environmental Career Opportunities* (http://ecojobs.com), that post internship and job positions. The Web site, Environmental Career Center (http://environmentalcareer.com) also offers job listings.

Read books and magazines about nature and the career of naturalists. Here are two book suggestions: *Steve & Me: Life with the Crocodile Hunter,* by Terri Irwin (Simon Spotlight Entertainment, 2008) and *A Naturalist and Other Beasts: Tales from a Life in the Field,* by George B. Schaller (Sierra Club Books/Counterpoint, 2010). One interesting magazine is *The American Naturalist,* published by the University of Chicago Press for the American Society of Naturalists. Visit http://www.jstor.org/action/showPublication?journalCode=amernatu to read sample articles.

EMPLOYERS

Naturalists may be employed by state agencies such as departments of wildlife, departments of fish and game, or departments of natural resources. They may work at the federal level for the U.S. Fish and Wildlife Service or the National Park Service. Naturalists may also work in the private sector for such employers as nature centers, arboretums, and botanical gardens.

STARTING OUT

If you hope to become a park employee, the usual method of entry is through part-time or seasonal employment for the first several jobs, then a full-time position. Because it is difficult to get experience before completing a college degree, and because seasonal employment is common, you should prepare to seek supplemental income for your first few years in the field.

International experience is helpful with agencies that work beyond the U.S. borders. This can be through the Peace Corps or other volunteer organizations that work with local populations on land and habitat management or restoration. Other volunteer experience is available through local restoration programs on sites in your area. Organizations such as The Nature Conservancy (http://www.nature.org), the Trust for Public Land (http://www.tpl.org), and many others buy land to restore, and these organizations rely extensively on volunteer labor for stewarding and working the land. Rescue and release centers work with injured and abandoned wildlife to rehabilitate them. Opportunities at these centers can include banding wild animals for tracking, working with injured or adolescent animals for release training, and adapting unreleasable animals to educational programs and presentations.

ADVANCEMENT

In some settings, such as small nature centers, there may be little room for advancement. In larger organizations, experience and additional education can lead to increased responsibility and pay. Among the higher level positions is that of director, handling supervisory, administrative, and public relations tasks.

Advancement into upper-level management and supervisory positions usually requires a graduate degree, although people with a graduate degree and no work experience will still have to start in nearly entry-level positions. So you can either work a few years and then return to school to get an advanced degree or complete your education and start in the same position as you would have without the degree. The advanced degree will allow you eventually to move further up in the organizational structure.

EARNINGS

Earnings for naturalists are influenced by several factors, including the naturalist's specific job (for example, a wildlife biologist, a water and soil conservationist, or a game manager), the employer (for example, a state or federal agency), and the naturalist's experience and education. The U.S. Fish and Wildlife Service reports that biologists working for this department have starting salaries at the GS-5 to GS-7 levels on the federal government pay scale. In 2010, biologists at the GS-5 pay level earned annual salaries that ranged from $27,431 to $35,657, and those at the GS-7 level earned annual salaries that ranged from $33,979 to $44,176. The U.S. Fish and

Wildlife Service further reports that biologists can expect to advance to GS-11 or GS-12 levels. In 2010, basic yearly pay at these levels was $50,287 and $60,274, respectively. In general, those working for state agencies have somewhat lower earnings, particularly at the entry level. And, again, the specific job a naturalist performs affects earnings. For example, the U.S. Department of Labor reports that conservation scientists had a median annual salary of $60,160 in 2009. However, some conservation workers put in 40-hour weeks and make less than $20,000 annually. As with other fields, management positions are among the highest paying. Salaries for managers may range from $45,000 to $75,000 or more annually. Keep in mind, though, that this position and these earnings are at the top of the field. The candidate who meets the qualifications for this position would have extensive experience and be responsible for, among other things, managing research programs statewide, hiring lower level managers, prioritizing and directing research, and acting as the department representative to other government agencies and public groups.

For some positions, housing and vehicles may be provided. Other benefits, depending on employer, may include health insurance, vacation time, and retirement plans.

WORK ENVIRONMENT

Field naturalists spend a majority of their working hours outdoors. Depending on the location, the naturalist must work in a wide variety of weather conditions: from frigid cold to sweltering heat to torrential rain. Remote sites are common, and long periods of working either in isolation or in small teams is not uncommon for field research and management. Heavy lifting, hauling, working with machinery and hand tools, digging, planting, harvesting, and tracking may fall to the naturalist working in the field. One wildlife manager in Montana spent every daylight hour for several days in a row literally running up and down snow-covered mountains, attempting to tranquilize and collar a mountain lion. Clearly, this can be a physically demanding job.

Indoor work includes scheduling, planning, and classroom teaching. Data gathering and maintaining logs and records are required for many jobs. Naturalists may need to attend and speak at local community meetings. They may have to read detailed legislative bills to analyze the impact of legislation before it becomes law.

Those in supervisory positions, such as directors, are often so busy with administrative and organizational tasks that they may spend little of their workday outdoors. Work that includes guided tours and walks through nature areas is frequently seasonal and usually dependent on daily visitors.

Full-time naturalists usually work about 35 to 40 hours per week. Overtime is often required, and for those naturalists working in areas visited by campers, camping season is extremely busy and can require much overtime. Wildlife and range managers may be on call during storms and severe weather. Seasonal work, such as burn season for land managers and stewards, may require overtime and frequent weekend work.

Naturalists have special occupational hazards, such as working with helicopters, small airplanes, all-terrain vehicles, and other modes of transport through rugged landscapes and into remote regions. Adverse weather conditions and working in rough terrain make illness and injury more likely. Naturalists must be able to get along with the variety of people using the area and may encounter armed individuals who are poaching or otherwise violating the law.

Working as a naturalist also provides a number of unique benefits. Most prominent is the chance to live and work in some of the most beautiful places in the world. For many individuals, the lower salaries are offset by the recreational and lifestyle opportunities afforded by living and working in such scenic areas. In general, occupational stress is low, and most naturalists appreciate the opportunity to continually learn about and work to improve the environment.

OUTLOOK

The employment outlook for naturalists is expected to be fair in the next decade. While a growing public concern about environmental issues may cause an increased demand for naturalists, this trend could be offset by government cutbacks in funding for nature programs. Reduced government spending on education may indirectly affect the demand for naturalists, as school districts would have less money to spend on outdoor education and recreation. Despite the limited number of available positions, the number of well-qualified applicants is expected to remain high.

FOR MORE INFORMATION

For information on careers, contact
American Society of Naturalists
http://www.asnamnat.org

For information about career opportunities, contact
Bureau of Land Management
U.S. Department of the Interior
1849 C Street, Room 5665
Washington, DC 20240-0001
Tel: 202-208-3801
http://www.blm.gov

For information on environmental expeditions, contact
Earthwatch Institute
114 Western Avenue
Boston, MA 02134-1037
Tel: 800-776-0188
E-mail: info@earthwatch.org
http://www.earthwatch.org

*This group offers internships and fellowships for college and gradu-
ate students with an interest in environmental issues. For information, contact*
Friends of the Earth
1100 15th Street, NW, 11th Floor
Washington, DC 20005-1707
Tel: 877-843-8687
http://www.foe.org

*This is a membership organization for people and organizations that
are committed to "conserving and restoring natural ecosystems,
focusing on birds, other wildlife, and their habitats for the benefit of
humanity and the earth's biological diversity." Visit its Web site for
detailed information and illustrations of birds in the United States
and an overview of its programs.*
National Audubon Society
225 Varick Street, 7th Floor
New York, NY 10014-4396
Tel: 212-979-3000
http://www.audubon.org

For information on a variety of conservation programs, contact
National Wildlife Federation
11100 Wildlife Center Drive
Reston, VA 20190-5362
Tel: 800-822-9919
http://www.nwf.org

For information on volunteer opportunities, contact
Student Conservation Association
689 River Road
PO Box 550
Charlestown, NH 03603-0550
Tel: 603-543-1700
http://www.thesca.org

For information on careers, contact
U.S. Fish and Wildlife Service
U.S. Department of the Interior
Division of Human Resources
4401 North Fairfax Drive, Mailstop: 2000
Arlington, VA 22203-1610
Tel: 800-344-8342
http://www.fws.gov/jobs

The society seeks to save wildlife and wild lands. Visit its Web site to learn more about programs for teens and to read sample articles from Wildlife Conservation Magazine.
Wildlife Conservation Society
2300 Southern Boulevard
Bronx, NY 10460-1068
Tel: 718-220-5100
http://www.wcs.org

The Wildlife Society *offers* Careers in Wildlife Conservation, *which details more than 10 careers in the field. The publication is available at its Web site, along with information on other publications, student chapters, certification, and membership for college students or anyone who is interested in wildlife conservation and management.*
The Wildlife Society
5410 Grosvenor Lane, Suite 200
Bethesda, MD 20814-2144
Tel: 301-897-9770
E-mail: TWS@wildlife.org
http://joomla.wildlife.org

Park Rangers

OVERVIEW

Park rangers enforce laws and regulations in national, state, and county parks. They help care for and maintain parks as well as inform, guide, and ensure the safety of park visitors.

HISTORY

Congress started the National Park System in the United States in 1872 when Yellowstone National Park was created. The National Park Service (NPS), a bureau of the U.S. Department of the Interior, was created in 1916 to preserve, protect, and manage the national, cultural, historical, and recreational areas of the National Park System. At that time, the park system contained less than 1 million acres. Today, the country's national parks cover more than 84 million acres of mountains, plains, deserts, swamps, historic sites, lakeshores, forests, rivers, battlefields, memorials, archaeological properties, and recreation areas.

All NPS areas are given one of the following designations: National Park, National Historical Park, National Battlefield, National Battlefield Park, National Battlefield Site, National Military Site, National Memorial, National Historic Site, National Monument, National Preserve, National Seashore, National Parkway, National Lakeshore, National Reserve, National River, National Wild and Scenic River, National Recreation Area, or just Park. (The White House in Washington, D.C., for example, which is administered by the NPS, is officially a Park.)

To protect the fragile, irreplaceable resources located in these areas, and to protect the millions of visitors who climb, ski, hike,

Facts About State Parks

- Total park visits each year: more than 725 million
- Number of state park units: 6,624
- Miles of trails: 41,725
- Total economic impact on communities: more than $20 billion a year

Source: National Association of State Park Directors

boat, fish, and otherwise explore them, the NPS employs park rangers. State and county parks employ rangers to perform similar tasks.

THE JOB

Park rangers have a wide variety of duties that range from conservation efforts to bookkeeping. Their first responsibility is, however, safety. Rangers who work in parks with treacherous terrain, dangerous wildlife (such as buffalo, grizzly bears, and mountain lions), or severe weather must make sure hikers, campers, and backpackers follow outdoor safety codes. They often require visitors to register at park offices so that rangers will know when someone does not return from a hike or climb and may be hurt. Rangers often participate in search-and-rescue missions for visitors who are lost or injured in parks. In mountainous or forested regions, they may use helicopters or horses for searches.

Rangers also protect parks from inappropriate use and other threats from humans. They register vehicles and collect parking and registration fees, which are used to help maintain roads and facilities. They enforce the laws, regulations, and policies of the parks, patrolling to prevent vandalism, theft, and harm to wildlife. Rangers may arrest and evict people who violate these laws. Some of their efforts to conserve and protect park resources include keeping jeeps and other motorized vehicles off sand dunes and other fragile lands. They make sure visitors do not litter, pollute water, chop down trees for firewood, or start unsafe campfires that could lead to catastrophic forest fires. When forest fires do start, rangers often help with the dangerous task of putting them out.

Park rangers carry out various tasks associated with the management of the natural resources within our National Park System. An important aspect of this responsibility is the care and management of both native and exotic animal species found within the boundaries of the parks. Duties may include conducting basic research, as well as disseminating information about the reintroduction of native animal populations and the protection of the natural habitat that supports the animals.

Rangers also help with conservation, research, and ecology efforts that are not connected to visitors' use of the park. They may study wildlife behavior patterns, for example, by tagging and following certain animals. In this way, they can chart the animals' migration patterns, assess the animals' impact on the park's ecosystem, and determine whether the park should take measures to control or encourage certain wildlife populations.

Some rangers study plant life and may work with conservationists to reintroduce native or endangered species. They measure the quality of water and air in the park to monitor and mitigate the effects of pollution and other threats from sources outside park boundaries.

In addition, park rangers help visitors enjoy and experience parks. In historical and other cultural parks, such as the Alamo in San Antonio, Texas, Independence Hall in Philadelphia, and the Lincoln Home in Springfield, Illinois, rangers give lectures and provide guided tours explaining the history and significance of the site. In natural parks, they may lecture on conservation topics, provide information about plants and animals in the park, and take visitors on interpretive walks, pointing out the area's flora, fauna, and geological characteristics. At a Civil War battlefield park, such as Gettysburg National Military Park in Pennsylvania or Vicksburg National Military Park in Mississippi, they explain to visitors what happened at that site during the Civil War and its implications for our country.

Park rangers are also indispensable to the management and administration of parks. They issue permits to visitors and vehicles and help plan the recreational activities in parks. They help in the planning and managing of park budgets. They keep records and compile statistics concerning weather conditions, resource conservation activities, and the number of park visitors.

Many rangers supervise other workers in the parks who build and maintain park facilities, work part time or seasonally, or operate concession facilities. Rangers often have their own park maintenance responsibilities, such as trail building, landscaping, and caring for visitor centers.

In some parks, rangers are specialists in certain areas of park protection, safety, or management. For example, in areas with heavy snowfalls and a high incidence of avalanches, experts in avalanche control and snow safety are designated *snow rangers*. They monitor snow conditions and patrol park areas to make sure visitors are not lost in snowslides.

REQUIREMENTS

High School

To prepare for the necessary college course load, you should take courses in earth science, biology, mathematics, English, and speech. Any classes or activities that deal with plant and animal life, the weather, geography, and interacting with others will be helpful.

Postsecondary Training

Employment as a federal or state park ranger requires either a college degree or a specific amount of education and experience. Approximately 100 bachelor's degree programs in parks and recreation management are accredited by the National Recreation and Park Association. To meet employment requirements, students in other relevant college programs must accumulate at least 24 semester hours of academic credit in park recreation and management, history, behavioral sciences, forestry, botany, geology, or other applicable subject areas.

Without a degree, you will need three years of experience in parks or conservation and you must show an understanding of what is required in park work. In addition, you must demonstrate good communications skills. A combination of education and experience can also fulfill job requirements, with one academic year of study equaling nine months of experience. Also, the orientation and training a ranger receives on the job may be supplemented with formal training courses.

To succeed as a ranger, you will need skills in protecting forests, parks, and wildlife and in interpreting natural or historical resources. Law enforcement and management skills are also important. If you wish to move into management positions, you may need a graduate degree. Approximately 50 universities offer master's degrees in park recreation and management and 16 have doctoral programs.

Other Requirements

In order to be a good park ranger, you should believe in the importance of the country's park resources and the mission of the park system. If you enjoy working outdoors, independently and with others, you may enjoy park ranger work. Rangers need self-confidence, patience, and the ability to stay levelheaded during emergencies. To participate in rescues, you need courage, physical stamina, and endurance, and to deal with visitors you must have tact, sincerity, a personable nature, and a sense of humor. A sense of camaraderie among fellow rangers also can add to the enjoyment of being a park ranger.

EXPLORING

If you are interested in exploring park ranger work, you may wish to apply for part-time or seasonal work in national, state, or county parks. Such workers usually perform maintenance and other unskilled tasks, but they have opportunities to observe park rangers and talk with them about their work. You might also choose to work as a volunteer. Many park research activities, study projects, and rehabilitation efforts are conducted by volunteer groups affiliated with universities or conservation organizations, and these activities can provide insight into the work done by park rangers.

EMPLOYERS

Park rangers in the NPS are employed by the U.S. Department of the Interior. Approximately 16,000 people work full time for the NPS; the NPS hires an additional 10,000 temporary and seasonal employees each year. Some rangers may be employed by other federal agencies or by state and county agencies in charge of their respective parks.

STARTING OUT

Many workers enter national park ranger jobs after working part time or seasonally at different parks. These workers often work at information desks or in fire control or law enforcement positions. Some help maintain trails, collect trash, or perform forestry activities. If you are interested in applying for a park ranger job with the federal government, contact your local Federal Job Information Center or the federal Office of Personnel Management (http://www.usajobs.gov) in Washington, D.C., for application information. To find jobs in state parks, you should write to the appropriate state departments for information.

ADVANCEMENT

Nearly all rangers start in entry-level positions, which means that nearly all higher level openings are filled by the promotion of current workers. Entry-level rangers may move into positions as district ranger or park manager, or they may become specialists in resource management or park planning. Rangers who show management skills and become park managers may move into administrative positions in the district, regional, or national headquarters.

The orientation and training a ranger receives on the job may be supplemented with formal training courses. Training for job skills unique to the National Park Service is available at the Horace M. Albright Training Center at Grand Canyon National Park in Arizona and the Stephen T. Mather Training Center at Harpers Ferry, West Virginia. In addition, training is available at the Federal Law Enforcement Training Center in Glynco, Georgia.

EARNINGS

Rangers in the NPS are usually hired at the GS-5 grade level, with a base salary of $27,431 in 2010. More experienced or educated rangers may enter the Park Service at the GS-9 level, which paid $41,563 to start. The average ranger is generally at about the second step of the GS-7 level, which translated to a salary of $35,112 in 2010. The most experienced rangers earned $44,176, the highest salary step in the G-7 level.

To move beyond this level, most rangers must become supervisors, subdistrict rangers, district rangers, or division chiefs. At these higher levels, people can earn more than $90,000 per year. These positions are difficult to obtain, however, because the turnover rate for positions above the GS-7 level is exceptionally low. The government may provide housing to rangers who work in remote areas.

Rangers in state parks work for the state government. According to Payscale.com, rangers employed by state parks earned salaries ranging from $21,036 to $38,515 in 2011. They receive comparable salaries and benefits, including paid vacations, sick leave, paid holidays, health and life insurance, and pension plans.

WORK ENVIRONMENT

Rangers work in parks all over the country, from the Okefenokee Swamp in Florida to Rocky Mountain National Park in Colorado. They work in the mountains and forests of Hawaii, Alaska, and California and in urban and suburban parks throughout the United States.

National park rangers are hired to work 40 hours per week, but their actual working hours can be long and irregular, with a great deal of overtime. They may receive extra pay or time off for working overtime. Some rangers are on call 24 hours a day for emergencies. During the peak tourist seasons, rangers work longer hours. Although many rangers work in offices, many also work outside in all kinds of climates and weather, and most work in a combination of the two settings. Workers may be called upon to risk their own health to rescue injured visitors in cold, snow, rain, and darkness. Rangers in Alaska must adapt to long daylight hours in the summer and short daylight hours in the winter. Working outdoors in beautiful surroundings, however, can be wonderfully stimulating and rewarding for the right kind of worker.

OUTLOOK

Park ranger jobs are scarce and competition for them is fierce. The NPS has reported that the ratio of applicants to available positions is sometimes as high as 100 to one. As a result, applicants should attain the greatest number and widest variety of applicable skills possible. They may wish to study subjects they can use in other fields: forestry, land management, conservation, wildlife management, history, and natural sciences, for example.

The scarcity of openings is expected to continue indefinitely. Job seekers, therefore, may wish to apply for outdoor work with agencies other than the NPS, including other federal land and resource management agencies and similar state and local agencies. Such agencies usually have more openings.

FOR MORE INFORMATION

For information about state parks and employment opportunities, contact
National Association of State Park Directors
8829 Woodyhill Road
Raleigh, NC 27613-1134
Tel: 919-676-8365
E-mail: NASPD@me.com
http://www.naspd.org

For general career information, contact
National Parks Conservation Association
777 6th Street, NW, Suite 700

Washington, DC 20001-3723
Tel: 800-628-7275
E-mail: npca@npca.org
http://www.npca.org

*For information about careers, job openings, and national parks,
contact*
National Park Service
1849 C Street, NW
Washington, DC 20240-0001
Tel: 202-208-6843
http://www.nps.gov

For information on postsecondary training programs, contact
National Recreation and Park Association
22377 Belmont Ridge Road
Ashburn, VA 20148-4501
Tel: 800-626-6772
http://www.nrpa.org

For information on volunteer opportunities, contact
Student Conservation Association
689 River Road
PO Box 550
Charlestown, NH 03603-0550
Tel: 603-543-1700
http://www.thesca.org

Pet Groomers

QUICK FACTS

School Subjects
Art
Business
Health

Personal Skills
Artistic
Helping/teaching

Work Environment
Indoors and outdoors
Primarily one location

Minimum Education Level
High school diploma

Salary Range
$15,590 to $19,550 to
$31,660+

Certification or Licensing
Voluntary

Outlook
Much faster than the average

DOT
418

GOE
03.02.01

NOC
0651, 6483

O*NET-SOC
39-2021.00

OVERVIEW

Pet groomers comb, cut, trim, and shape the fur of all types of dogs and cats. They comb out the animal's fur and trim the hair to the proper style for the size and breed. They also trim the animal's nails, bathe it, and dry its hair. In the process, they check for flea or tick infestation and any visible health problems. In order to perform these grooming tasks, the pet groomer must be able to calm the animal down and gain its confidence. In addition to dogs and cats, groomers are also called upon to tend to more exotic pets these days, such as ferrets, birds, and reptiles.

HISTORY

As long as dog has been man's best friend, humans have been striving to keep their animal companions healthy and happy. Pets are often considered members of the family and are treated as such. Just as parents take their children to the doctor for vaccinations and to the barber for haircuts, pets are often treated to regular veterinarian visits and grooming services.

An increasingly urban society and higher standards of living can both be considered significant factors in the growing number of professional grooming establishments in this country. City dwellers who live in small apartments have less space to groom their pets than their farm-dwelling forebears had. Many busy professionals have neither the time nor the inclination to learn the proper techniques and purchase the tools needed for grooming. Additionally, many apartment and condominium buildings have

A groomer gives a Wheaton terrier a bath before trimming its hair.
(Syracuse Newspapers, David Lassman, The Image Works)

regulations to which pet owners must adhere in order to ensure the safety and comfort of tenants. In compact living quarters, people don't want to encounter smelly pups in the hallway. Also, the rise of multiple-income families and an increased standard of living gives animal aficionados the disposable income to pamper their pets with professional grooming services.

New developments in animal grooming include high-performance clippers and cutting tools and more humane restraining devices. Current trends toward specialized services include perfuming, powdering, styling, and even massage, aromatherapy, and tattooing for pets.

THE JOB

Although all dogs and cats benefit from regular grooming, shaggy, longhaired dogs give pet groomers the bulk of their business. Some types of dogs need regular grooming for their standard appearance; among this group are poodles, schnauzers, cocker spaniels, and many types of terriers. Show dogs, or dogs that are shown in competition, are groomed frequently. Before beginning grooming,

Learn More About It

Hayhurst, Chris. *Cool Careers Without College for Animal Lovers.* New York: Rosen Publishing Group, 2002.

Hollow, Michele C., and William P. Rives. *The Everything Guide to Working with Animals: From Dog Groomer to Wildlife Rescuer—Tons of Great Jobs for Animal Lovers.* Cincinnati, Ohio: Adams Media Corporation, 2009.

Lee, Mary Price. *Opportunities in Animal and Pet Careers.* 2d ed. New York: McGraw-Hill, 2008.

Miller, Louise. *Careers for Animal Lovers and Other Zoological Types.* 3d ed. New York: McGraw-Hill, 2007.

Nigro, Joseph. *101 Best Businesses for Pet Lovers.* Naperville, Ill.: Sphinx Publishing, 2007.

Shenk, Ellen. *Careers with Animals: Exploring Occupations Involving Dogs, Horses, Cats, Birds, Wildlife, and Exotics.* Mechanicsburg, Pa.: Stackpole Books, 2005.

the dog groomer talks with the owner to find out the style of cut that the dog is to have. The dog groomer also relies on experience to determine how a particular breed of dog is supposed to look.

The dog groomer places the animal on a grooming table. To keep the dog steady during the clipping, a nylon collar or noose, which hangs from an adjustable pole attached to the grooming table, is slipped around its neck. The dog groomer talks to the dog or uses other techniques to keep the animal calm and gain its trust. If the dog doesn't calm down but snaps and bites instead, the groomer may have to muzzle it. If a dog is completely unmanageable, the dog groomer may ask the owner to have the dog tranquilized by a veterinarian before grooming.

After calming the dog, the groomer brushes it and tries to untangle its hair. If the dog's hair is very overgrown or is very shaggy such as an English sheepdog's, the groomer may have to cut away part of its coat with scissors before beginning any real grooming. Brushing the coat is good for both longhaired and shorthaired dogs as brushing removes shedding hair and dead skin. It also neatens the coat so the groomer can tell from the shape and proportions of the dog how to cut its hair in the most attractive way. Hair that is severely matted is actually painful to the animal because the mats pull at the animal's skin. Having these mats removed is necessary to the animal's health and comfort.

Once the dog is brushed, the groomer cuts and shapes the dog's coat with electric clippers. Next, the dog's ears are cleaned and its nails are trimmed. The groomer must take care not to cut the nails too short because they may bleed and cause the dog pain. If the nails do bleed, a special powder is applied to stop the bleeding. The comfort of the animal is an important concern for the groomer.

The dog is then given a bath, sometimes by a worker known as a *dog bather*. The dog is lowered into a stainless steel tub, sprayed with warm water, scrubbed with a special shampoo, and rinsed. This may be repeated several times if the dog is very dirty. The dog groomer has special chemicals that can be used to deodorize a dog that has encountered a skunk or has gone for a swim in foul water. If a dog has fleas or ticks, the dog groomer treats them at this stage by soaking the wet coat with a solution to kill the insects. This toxic solution must be kept out of the dog's eyes, ears, and nose, which may be cleaned more carefully with a sponge or washcloth. A hot oil treatment may also be applied to condition the dog's coat.

The groomer dries the dog after bathing, either with a towel, hand-held electric blower, or in a drier cage with electric blow driers. Poodles and some other types of dogs have their coats fluff-dried, then scissored for the final pattern or style. Poodles, which at one time were the mainstay of the dog grooming business, generally take the longest to groom because of their intricate clipping pattern. Most dogs can be groomed in about 90 minutes, although grooming may take several hours for shaggier breeds whose coats are badly matted and overgrown.

More and more cats, especially longhaired breeds, are now being taken to pet groomers. The procedure for cats is the same as for dogs, although cats are not dipped when bathed. As the dog or cat is groomed, the groomer checks to be sure there are no signs of disease in the animal's eyes, ears, skin, or coat. If there are any abnormalities, such as bald patches or skin lesions, the groomer tells the owner and may recommend that a veterinarian check the animal. The groomer may also give the owner tips on animal hygiene.

Pet owners and those in pet care generally have respect for pet groomers who do a good job and treat animals well. Many people, especially those who raise show dogs, grow to rely on particular pet groomers to do a perfect job each time. Pet groomers can earn satisfaction from taking a shaggy, unkempt animal and transforming it into a beautiful creature. On the other hand, some owners may unfairly blame the groomer if the animal becomes ill while in the groomer's care or for some malady or condition that is not the groomer's fault.

Because they deal with both the pets and their owners, pet groomers can find their work both challenging and rewarding. One owner of a grooming business asserts, "Nothing feels better than developing a relationship with pets and their owners. It's almost like they become an extended part of the family. When working with living animals you accept the responsibility of caring for them to the best of your ability, and the rewards are great. I don't think that can be said of a mechanic or furnace repairman."

REQUIREMENTS

High School

A high school diploma generally is not required for people working as pet groomers. A diploma or GED certificate, however, can be a great asset to people who would like to advance within their present company or move to other careers in animal care that require more training, such as veterinary technicians. Useful courses include English, business math, general science, anatomy and physiology, health, zoology, psychology, bookkeeping, office management, typing, art, and first aid.

Postsecondary Training

A person interested in pet grooming can be trained for the field in one of three ways: enrolling in a pet grooming school; working in a pet shop or kennel and learning on the job; or reading one of the many books on pet grooming and practicing on his or her own pet.

To enroll in most pet grooming schools, a person must be at least 17 years old and fond of animals. Programs typically last from two to 18 weeks. Previous experience in pet grooming can sometimes be applied for course credits. Students study a wide range of topics including the basics of bathing, brushing, and clipping, the care of ears and nails, coat and skin conditions, animal anatomy terminology, and sanitation. They also study customer relations, which is very important for those who plan to operate their own shops. During training, students practice their techniques on actual animals, which people bring in for grooming at a discount rate. You can access a list of pet grooming schools by visiting http://www.petgroomer.com. Many other grooming schools advertise in dog and pet magazines. It is important for students to choose an accredited, state-licensed school in order to increase both their employment opportunities and professional knowledge.

Students can also learn pet grooming while working in an informal internship at a grooming shop, kennel, animal hospital, or veterinarian's office. The internship typically lasts six to 10 weeks. They usually begin with tasks such as shampooing dogs and cats, and trimming their nails, then gradually work their way up to brushing and basic haircuts. With experience, they may learn more difficult cuts and use these skills to earn more pay or start their own business.

The essentials of pet grooming can also be learned from any of several good books available on grooming. These books contain all the information a person needs to know to start his or her own pet grooming business, including the basic cuts, bathing and handling techniques, and type of equipment needed. Still, many of the finer points of grooming, such as the more complicated cuts and various safety precautions, are best learned while working under an experienced groomer. There still is no substitute for on-the-job training and experience.

Certification or Licensing

Presently, state licensing or certification is not required, and there are no established labor unions for pet groomers. To start a grooming salon or other business, a license is needed from the city or town in which a person plans to practice. The National Dog Groomers Association of America offers certification to groomers who pass written and practical examinations. The Pet Care Services Association, the International Society of Canine Cosmetologists, and the International Association of Canine Professionals also offer certification.

Other Requirements

The primary qualification for a person who wants to work with pets is a love of animals. Animals can sense when someone does not like them or is afraid of them. A person needs certain skills in order to work with nervous, aggressive, or fidgety animals. They must be patient with the animals, able to gain their respect, and enjoy giving the animals a lot of love and attention. Persistence and endurance are also helpful as grooming one animal can take several hours of strenuous work. Groomers should enjoy working with their hands and have good eyesight and manual dexterity to accurately cut a clipping pattern.

EXPLORING

To find out if you are suited for a job in pet grooming, you should familiarize yourself with animals as much as possible. This can be done in many ways, starting with the proper care of your dog, cat, or other family pet. You can also offer to tend to the pets of friends and neighbors to see how well you handle unfamiliar animals. Youth organizations such as the Boy Scouts, Girl Scouts, and 4-H Clubs sponsor projects that give members the chance to raise and care for animals. You can also volunteer or work part time caring for animals at an animal hospital, kennel, pet shop, animal shelter, nature center, or zoo.

EMPLOYERS

Grooming salons, kennels, pet shops, veterinary practices, animal hospitals, and grooming schools employ pet groomers. The pet business is thriving all over the country, and the opportunities for groomers are expected to increase steadily in the coming years. Although most employers can offer attractive benefits packages, many pet groomers choose to go into business for themselves rather than turn over 40 to 50 percent of their fees to their employers. Graduates of accredited pet grooming schools benefit from the schools' job placement services, which can help students find work in the kind of setting they prefer.

STARTING OUT

Graduates from dog grooming schools can take advantage of the schools' job placement services. Generally, there are more job openings than qualified groomers to fill them, so new graduates may have several job offers to consider. These schools learn of job openings in all parts of the United States and are usually happy to contact prospective employers and write letters of introduction for graduates.

The National Dog Groomers Association of America (NDGAA) also promotes professional identification through membership and certification testing throughout the United States and Canada. The NDGAA offers continuing education, accredited workshops, certification testing, seminars, insurance programs, a job placement program, membership directory, and other services and products. Other associations of interest to dog groomers are the Humane Society of the United States, Pet Care Services Association, and the United Kennel Club. Because dog groomers are concerned with the health and safety of the animals they service, membership in groups that promote and protect animal welfare is very common.

Other sources of job information include the classified ads of daily newspapers and listings in dog and pet magazines. Job leads may be available from private or state employment agencies or from referrals of salon or kennel owners. People looking for work should contact prospective employers, inform them of their qualifications, and, if invited, visit their establishments.

ADVANCEMENT

Pet groomers who work for other people may advance to a more responsible position such as office manager or dog trainer. If dog groomers start their own shops, they may become successful enough to expand or to open branch offices or area franchises. Skilled groomers may want to work for a dog grooming school as an instructor, possibly advancing to a job as a school director, placement officer, or other type of administrator.

The pet industry is booming, so there are many avenues of advancement for groomers who like to work with pets. With more education, a groomer may get a job as a veterinary technician or assistant at a shelter or animal hospital. Those who like to train dogs may open obedience schools, train guide dogs, work with field and hunting dogs, or even train stunt and movie dogs. People can also open their own kennels, breeding and pedigree services, gaming dog businesses, or pet supply distribution firms. Each of these requires specialized knowledge and experience, so additional study, education, and work is often needed.

EARNINGS

Groomers charge either by the job or the hour. If they are on the staff of a salon or work for another groomer, they get to keep 50 to 60 percent of the fees they charge. For this reason, many groomers branch off to start their own businesses. "I would never want to go back to working for someone else or giving up a commission on my groomings," says one owner-operator of a grooming business.

The U.S. Department of Labor (DOL) reports that median hourly earnings of nonfarm animal caretakers (the category in which pet groomers are classified) were $9.40 (or $19,550 annually) in 2009. Salaries ranged from less than $7.49 (or $15,590 annually) to more than $15.22 per hour (or $31,660 annually). Those who own and operate their own grooming services can earn significantly more, depending on how hard they work, the clientele they service, and the economy of the area in which they work.

Groomers generally buy their own clipping equipment, including barber's shears, brushes, and clippers. A new set of equipment costs around $325 to $400; used sets cost less. Groomers employed full time at salons, grooming schools, pet shops, animal hospitals, and kennels often get a full range of benefits, including paid vacations and holidays, medical and dental insurance, and retirement pensions.

WORK ENVIRONMENT

Salons, kennels, and pet shops, as well as gaming and breeding services, should be clean and well lighted, with modern equipment and clean surroundings. Establishments that do not meet these standards endanger the health of the animals that are taken there and the owners of these establishments should be reported. Groomers who are self-employed may work out of their homes. Some groomers buy vans and convert them into grooming shops. They drive them to the homes of the pets they work on, which many owners find very convenient. Those who operate these "groommobiles" may work on 30 or 40 dogs a week, and factor their driving time and expenses into their fees.

Groomers usually work a 40-hour week and may have to work evenings or weekends. Those who own their own shops or work out of their homes, like other self-employed people, work very long hours and may have irregular schedules. One groomer points out that, "You can't just decide to call in sick when you have seven dogs scheduled to be groomed that day. We have had midnight emergency calls from clients needing immediate help of one kind or another with their pet." Many groomers/business owners believe that the occasionally hectic schedule of the field is not always a negative aspect, since they take great pride in being able to offer personal service and care to both animals and clients.

Groomers are on their feet much of the day, and their work can get very tiring when they have to lift and restrain large animals. They must wear comfortable clothing that allows for freedom of movement, but they should also be presentable enough to deal with pet owners and other clients.

When working with any sort of animal, a person may encounter bites, scratches, strong odors, fleas, and other insects. They may have to deal with sick or bad-tempered animals. The groomer must regard every animal as a unique individual and treat it with respect. Groomers need to be careful while on the job, especially when handling flea and tick killers, which are toxic to humans as well as the pests.

OUTLOOK

Employment for animal caretakers (including pet groomers) is expected to grow much faster than the average for all careers through 2018, according to the DOL. Every year more people are keeping dogs and cats as pets. They are spending more money to pamper their animals, but often don't have enough free time or the inclination to groom their pets themselves. Grooming is not just a luxury for pets, however, because regular attention makes it more likely that any injury or illness will be noticed and treated.

Also, as nontraditional pets become more mainstream, innovative groomers will need to take advantage of new techniques and facilities for bringing animals other than dogs and cats into the pet salon.

FOR MORE INFORMATION

For more information about grooming and related professions, contact

Intergroom
76 Carol Drive
Dedham, MA 02026-6635
Tel: 781-326-3376
E-mail: intergroom@msn.com
http://www.intergroom.com

The association offers membership options for walkers, groomers, kennel owners, veterinarians, pet sitters, and other professionals in the dog world—including a membership category for those who have "an active interest in making a career within the canine profession, but do not yet have the experience to qualify for acceptance" at professional membership levels. Visit its Web site for information on membership, certification, training, and other topics.

International Association of Canine Professionals
Tel: 407-469-2008
E-mail: iacpadmin@mindspring.com
http://canineprofessionals.com

Contact the society for information on certification and training programs and workshops.

International Society of Canine Cosmetologists
2702 Covington Drive
Garland, TX 75040-3822
E-mail: iscc@petstylist.com
http://www.petstylist.com/ISCC/ISCCMain.htm

For information on shows, new grooming products and techniques, and workshop and certification test sites and dates, contact
National Dog Groomers Association of America
PO Box 101
Clark, PA 16113-0101
Tel: 724-962-2711
E-mail: ndga@nationaldoggroomers.com
http://www.nationaldoggroomers.com

This is a professional membership association for pet boarders, sitters, groomers, animal trainers, and pet suppliers. It offers a membership category for any "individual who is interested in the pet care industry, but who does not presently operate a non-veterinary pet care business." Visit the association's Web site for information on training opportunities, membership, certification, networking events, and pet health.
Pet Care Services Association
401 North Michigan Avenue, Suite 2200
Chicago, IL 60611-4245
Tel: 800-218-9123
http://www.petcareservices.org

Pet Shop Workers

OVERVIEW

Pet shop workers, from entry-level clerks to store managers, are involved in the daily upkeep of a pet store; they sell pets and pet supplies, including food, medicine, toys, carriers, and educational books and DVDs. They work with customers, answering questions and offering animal care advice. They keep the store, aquariums, and animal cages clean, and look after the health of the pets for sale. They also stock shelves, order products from distributors, and maintain records on the animals and products.

HISTORY

Can you imagine George Washington with a pet hamster? No? Well, there's a good reason for that—the hamster wasn't even domesticated until around 1930. But picturing George alongside his faithful steed isn't a problem at all. Just as successful horse-trading was important to the development of Indian villages for thousands of years, horse-trading proved a staple of American business from the first colonies to the cities of the early 20th century. Though the horses in the stables of the early Americans were well-loved by their owners, they weren't exactly considered "pets" or "companion animals." Horses were relied upon for transportation, industry, and farm work. But these horse traders, with their sense of business and knowledge of animal care, are early examples of the pet shop owners who found thriving business on the town squares across the developing country, alongside the apothecaries and general stores.

Typical Positions at Major Pet Chains

- Cashier
- Companion animal specialist
- Companion animal technician
- Department manager
- Groomer
- Sales associate
- Stock worker
- Team Leader
- Trainer

Though domestic cats in the United States only date from around 1750, they were first domesticated (along with lions and hyenas) around 1900 B.C. in Egypt. In the years before that, cats were considered sacred (perhaps explaining the royal bearing of many of today's pampered house cats!). Dogs as pets predate cats; ancient carvings and paintings depict a range of breeds, and Egyptian tomb paintings feature greyhounds and terriers.

THE JOB

The soft barks of the puppies being groomed in the back of the shop; the trills and whistles of the birds in their cages; the bubbling of the fish tanks—these sights and sounds combine to make a visit to the neighborhood pet store unlike any other shopping experience. But running a pet shop calls upon the same business skills required for the operation of any retail establishment. Pet shop workers are in the business to sell to customers; many pet stores employ cashiers, sales and marketing people, managers, and bookkeepers. Pet shop owners may also hire pet groomers, animal caretakers, and animal trainers. A pet shop must have a staff that loves animals, is knowledgeable about pets and their care, and is good with customers.

The top priorities for pet shop workers are animal care and customer care. Though the size of the pet shop will determine how many duties are assigned each worker, most pet shop workers take part in preparing the store for opening; they make sure the shop is clean, the shelves are in order, the aisles are clear, and the cash register is ready for sales. Cages and fish tanks are cleaned, and the animals are fed and watered. Though some pet shops continue to sell dogs and cats, most buyers for those kinds of animals purchase directly from breeders, or select animals from shelters. Today's pet shops generally specialize in birds, fish, and small animals such as hamsters and mice. Once the animals are taken care of, the pet shop workers see to the needs of the customers. "At a small pet shop, you begin to think of your customers as your friends," says Max Paterson, a high school student who works for a pet shop in Ohio. "I once tried to count how many questions I answered in a day, and when I got past 250, I stopped." Customers rely on pet shop workers for animal care advice, and expect them to be knowledgeable not only of the pets for sale, but of the food, medicines, and other supplies, as well. "The biggest benefits I've received from the job," Paterson says, "are the relationships with the customers, and the huge dictionary of tropical fish I've developed in my head."

Pet shops may offer a variety of services, including pet grooming, dog training, and animal boarding. They may also offer animal vaccinations. A *store manager* is often responsible for organizing the various services, interviewing and hiring store employees, dealing with distributors, and maintaining records of sales and animal health.

REQUIREMENTS

High School

For pet store work, you will need to develop a good business sense, an ability to work well with customers, and knowledge of animals and their care. In high school, accounting, marketing, and other business-related courses are valuable, as are math courses. You will need math for both money management and for figuring proper feed and medication amounts for the animals. The sciences are important for anyone working with animals. Knowledge of chemistry will come in handy when preparing medications and chemicals for the aquariums. Biology will introduce you to the biological systems of various kinds of animals. Geography courses can also add to your understanding of animals by introducing you to their natural habitats and origins.

A business club, such as Future Business Leaders of America (http://fbla-pbl.org), will introduce you to area business owners, and help you develop skills in advertising, marketing, and management. Participation in agricultural clubs and 4-H (http://www.4-h.org) can teach you about animal care and responsibilities.

Postsecondary Training

You can easily get work at a pet store without any college education or special training. As with most retail businesses, pet shops often employ high school students for part-time and summer positions. Store owners usually hire people with a love of animals, and some knowledge of their care, for entry-level positions such as clerk, cashier, and salesperson. For management positions, a pet shop owner may want someone with some higher education. It is also easier to advance into management positions if you have a college degree.

Though any college degree will be valuable for higher level pet shop positions, you'll want to take courses in marketing, accounting, merchandising, and other business-related areas. Some pet shops also like to hire people with veterinary tech training. Students pursuing a pre-veterinary sciences degree often work part time in a pet shop to gain experience with animals and their owners.

Because of the wide availability of retail work, you would be better advised to pursue a paid entry-level position at a store, rather than an internship. But belonging to a business organization as a student can offer you valuable insight into marketing and management. DECA (http://www.deca.org), an association of marketing students, is an organization that prepares high school and junior college students for retail careers. There are many local chapters of DECA across the country, and annual leadership conferences. Some DECA chapters also offer scholarships to marketing students.

Certification or Licensing

There is no specialized certification available for pet store workers. The National Retail Federation offers the following voluntary designations to sales workers who successfully pass an assessment and meet other requirements: national professional certification in sales, national professional certification in customer service, national professional certification in retail management, and the professional retail business credential. Contact the federation for more information.

No licensing is available for pet shop workers.

Other Requirements

"It takes a great deal of respect and love for animals," Max Paterson says about working in a pet shop, "a person who can help customers even when there are lots of them, and someone who's not afraid to get their hands dirty every now and again." As with any retail job, you must be prepared to serve people on a daily basis—you should be friendly and outgoing, and prepared to answer questions clearly and patiently. Though most of your encounters with these fellow animal lovers will likely be pleasant, you must be prepared for the occasional dissatisfied customer; dealing with angry customers requires you to remain calm, and to settle the dispute diplomatically. You must remain informed about new products and animal care; customers will be asking you about the right size cages for particular birds, or how many fish a tank can hold. In answering such questions, your first concern must be for the well-being of the animals, not for the biggest profit. Some customers may even be testing you with their questions, making sure the store's staff is reliable.

Depending on your duties at the pet store, you'll need analytical skills; you'll be analyzing data when ordering new products, choosing vendors, and examining sales figures and invoices. In whatever position you fill at the pet store, it will be important for you to manage your time well to deal with customers while keeping the store orderly and the shelves well stocked.

EXPLORING

With the number of volunteer opportunities at animal shelters, zoos, and other animal care facilities, you can easily gain experience working with animals. You may also want to spend a few days "shadowing" some pet shop managers, following them throughout their workday to get a sense of their duties. Max Paterson, before going to work for the pet shop, spent a lot of his spare time there learning about the animals and the products for sale. "The first step was creating a trusting, customer/owner relationship," he says. "From there, I began asking if he needed some odd jobs done for a few bucks, and in doing these jobs, and just hanging out at the store, I began to pick up on all he was saying to the customers. Soon, I too knew enough to help customers."

EMPLOYERS

Pet store workers work in pet stores—from "mom and pop" establishments to large chains such as PETCO, Petland, and PetSmart.

STARTING OUT

After spending so much time at his local pet shop, and learning so much about the business, Max Paterson was able to step into a job. "I now work regular hours," he says, "and have often been left to watch the store on my own." Experience with animal care can help you get a job in a pet store, but such experience is not always required. A pet shop owner or manager may be prepared to give you on-the-job training. You can check the classified ads in your local newspaper for pet shop jobs, but a better approach is to visit all the pet stores in your area and fill out applications. If you don't hear back from the store right away, follow up on a regular basis so that the manager or store owner gets to know you. That way, when there is a job opening, the manager will have you in mind.

For management positions, you should have some background in entry-level retail positions, and some college education. While pursuing that education, you can take part-time work in pet stores or other retail businesses. Though any retail experience is valuable, experience in a small pet store will involve you directly with many of the main concerns of a business; in a larger pet "megastore" your experience may be limited to a few duties.

ADVANCEMENT

The longer you work in one store, the more responsibilities you're likely to be given. After starting as a cashier, or stock person, you may eventually be allowed to open and close the store, place orders, create advertisements, order new products, and deal with distributors. Experience in the many different areas of one particular business can lead to advancement from an entry-level position to a management position, even if you don't have a college education.

As a manager, you may be allowed to expand the store in new directions; with the understanding of a store and its clientele, you can introduce such additions as an animal training program, sponsorship of adopt-a-pet and animal-assisted therapy programs, and new product lines.

EARNINGS

Entry-level pet shop workers earn minimum wage, and even those with experience probably won't make much more than that. Though the average store manager makes under $40,000, there does seem to be the possibility of salary increases in the future. In order to attract more experienced store managers, store owners are beginning to reward managers for their varied responsibilities and extra hours. The size of the store also makes a difference; stores with larger volumes pay their managers considerably more than stores with volumes of less than one million dollars. The size of the store also determines the number of benefits for a full-time employee. Benefits might include vacation days, sick leave, health and life insurance, and a savings and pension program.

The U.S. Department of Labor reports that in 2009, retail salespersons of all types had a median hourly wage of $9.74 ($20,260 annually), with wages ranging from less than $7.41 ($15,420 annually) to more than $18.49 ($38,460 annually). Retail managers had median annual salaries of $34,900. Managers of large stores with many employees earned more than $60,400 a year.

WORK ENVIRONMENT

A clean, healthy pet shop should make for a very comfortable work environment. But to keep the place clean and healthy, workers in this field handle animals, clean out cages and fish tanks, and prepare medications. They also sweep the floors of the store, and dust shelves. A pet shop should also be well ventilated and temperature controlled. During work hours, pet shop workers usually stay indoors and don't venture far from their assigned workstations.

Working in a public place devoted to the care of animals, some pet shop workers find themselves taking on extra responsibilities, such as providing foster care for abused or abandoned animals. Though pet shop workers do their best to educate customers and to prepare them for pet ownership, they must still deal with the fact that many animals in their community are without good homes.

OUTLOOK

The larger pet stores, which can afford to offer special pricing, inexpensive grooming facilities, and free training programs, are taking much of the business away from the smaller, traditional, "mom and pop" pet shops. This trend is likely to continue, but small stores will survive as they promote a more personalized and knowledgeable assistance not available from the larger stores. The pet retail industry, in some form, will grow along with the retail industry in general.

The puppies and kittens frolicking in the windows of corner pet shops are becoming a thing of the past as animal activists have made the public increasingly aware of "puppy mills" and other unregulated animal breeders. Groups such as the American Society for the Prevention of Cruelty to Animals fight for better regulation of animal sales practices and animal care in pet shops.

Holistic pet care is also changing the industry—nonchemical remedies, natural foods, and vitamin supplements for animals are gaining more acceptance from store owners, animal breeders, and veterinarians. And, as with every industry, computers have influenced the way stores keep records of business, sales, and animal health. Pet shop managers will be expected to have some computer skills and a basic understanding of bookkeeping software.

FOR MORE INFORMATION

For more information on the pet products industry, contact
American Pet Products Association
255 Glenville Road
Greenwich, CT 06831-4148
Tel: 203-532-0000
http://www.appma.org

For information about pet care, contact
American Society for the Prevention of Cruelty to Animals
424 East 92nd Street
New York, NY 10128-6804
Tel: 212-876-7700
http://www.aspca.org

For information on careers, visit the NRF Web site.
National Retail Federation (NRF)
325 7th Street, NW, Suite 1100
Washington, DC 20004-2825
Tel: 800-673-4692
http://www.nrf.com

Pet Sitters

OVERVIEW

When pet owners are on vacation or working long hours, they hire *pet sitters* to come to their homes and visit their animals. During short, daily visits, pet sitters feed the animals, play with them, clean up after them, give them medications when needed, and let them in and out of the house for exercise. *Dog walkers* may be responsible only for taking their clients' dogs out for exercise. Pet sitters may also be available for overnight stays, looking after the houses of clients as well as their pets.

HISTORY

Animals have been revered by humans for centuries, as is evidenced by early drawings on the walls of caves and tombs—cats were even considered sacred by the ancient Egyptians. Though these sacred cats may have had their own personal caretakers, it has only been within the last 10 to 15 years that pet sitting has evolved into a successful industry and a viable career option. Before groups such as the National Association of Professional Pet Sitters (NAPPS), which formed in 1989, and Pet Sitters International (PSI), which was founded in 1994, were developed, pet sitting was regarded as a way for people with spare time to make a little extra money on the side. Like babysitting, pet sitting attracted primarily teenagers and women; many children's books over the last century have depicted the trials and tribulations of young entrepreneurs in the business of pet sitting and dog walking. Patti Moran, the founder of both NAPPS and PSI, and author of *Pet Sitting for Profit*, is credited with helping pet sitters gain recognition

Pet Sitters Provide Extra Special Protection

Professional pet sitters do more than just take care of pets; they also help protect homes from theft. They do this by

- turning on different lamps at different times
- opening and closing curtains and blinds
- arriving in unmarked cars
- wearing everyday attire
- bringing in newspapers and mail

as successful small business owners. Though many people still only pet sit occasionally for neighbors and friends, others are developing long lists of clientele and proving strong competition to kennels and boarding facilities.

THE JOB

If you live in a big city, you have seen them hit the streets with their packs of dogs. Dragged along by four or five leashes, the pet sitter walks the dogs down the busy sidewalks, allowing the animals their afternoon exercise while the pet owners are stuck in the office. You may not have realized it, but those dog walkers are probably the owners of thriving businesses. Though a hobby for some, pet sitting is for others a demanding career with many responsibilities. Michele Finley is one of these pet sitters, in the Park Slope neighborhood of Brooklyn, New York. "A lot of people seem to think pet sitting is a walk in the park (pun intended)," she says, "and go into it without realizing what it entails (again)."

For those who cannot bear to leave their dogs or cats at kennels or boarders while they are away, pet sitters offer peace of mind to the owners, as well as their pets. With a pet sitter, pets can stay in familiar surroundings, as well as avoid the risks of illnesses passed on by other animals. The pets are also assured routine exercise and no disruptions in their diets. Most pet sitters prefer to work only with cats and dogs, but pet sitters are also called upon to care for birds, reptiles, gerbils, fish, and other animals.

With their own set of keys, pet sitters let themselves into the homes of their clients and care for their animals while they're away at work or on vacation. Pet sitters feed the animals, make sure they have water, and give them their medications. They clean up any messes the animals have made and clean litter boxes. They give the animals attention, playing with them, letting them outside, and taking them for walks. Usually, a pet sitter can provide pet owners with a variety of personal pet care services—they may take a pet to the vet, offer grooming, sell pet-related products, and give advice. Some pet sitters take dogs out into the country, to mountain parks, or to lakes, for exercise in wide-open spaces. "You should learn to handle each pet as an individual," Finley advises. "Just because Fluffy likes his ears scratched doesn't mean Spot does."

Pet sitters typically plan one to three visits (of 30 to 60 minutes in length) per day, or they may make arrangements to spend the night. In addition to caring for the animals, pet sitters also look after the houses of their clients. They bring in the newspapers and the mail; they water the plants; they make sure the house is securely locked. Pet sitters generally charge by the hour or per visit. They may also have special pricing for overtime, emergency situations, extra duties, and travel.

Most pet sitters work alone, without employees, no matter how demanding the work. Though this means getting to keep all the money, it also means keeping all the responsibilities. A successful pet sitting service requires a fair amount of business management. Finley works directly with the animals from 10:00 A.M. until 5:00 or 6:00 P.M., with no breaks; upon returning home, she will have five to 10 phone messages from clients. Part of her evening then consists of scheduling and rescheduling appointments, offering advice on feeding, training, and other pet care concerns, and giving referrals for boarders and vets. But despite these hours, and despite having to work holidays, as well as days when she's not feeling well, Finley appreciates many things about the job. "Being with the furries all day is the best," she says. She also likes not having to dress up for work and not having to commute to an office.

REQUIREMENTS

High School

As a pet sitter, you will be running your own business all by yourself; therefore you should take high school courses such as accounting, marketing, and office skills. Computer science will help you learn about the software you'll need for managing accounts and scheduling. Join a school business group that will introduce you to business practices and local entrepreneurs.

Science courses such as biology and chemistry, as well as health courses, will give you some good background for developing animal care skills. As a pet sitter, you will be overseeing the health of the animals, their exercise, and their diets. You will also be preparing medications and administering eye and ear drops.

As a high school student, you can easily gain hands-on experience as a pet sitter. If you know anyone in your neighborhood with pets, volunteer to care for the animals whenever the owners go on vacation. Once you've got experience and a list of references, you may even be able to start a part-time job for yourself as a pet sitter.

Postsecondary Training

Many pet sitters start their own businesses after having gained experience in other areas of animal care. Vet techs and pet shop workers may promote their animal care skills to develop a clientele for more profitable pet sitting careers. Graduates from a business college may recognize pet sitting as a great way to start a business with little overhead. But neither a vet tech qualification nor a business degree is required to become a successful pet sitter. And the only special training you need to pursue is actual experience. A local pet shop or chapter of the American Society for the Prevention of Cruelty to Animals may offer seminars in various aspects of animal care; the NAPPS offers a mentorship program, as well as a newsletter, while PSI sponsors correspondence programs and teleconferences.

Certification or Licensing

Pet Sitters International offers the accredited pet sitter designation to applicants who pass an open book examination that covers topics in four major categories: Pet Care, Health and Nutrition, Business and Office Procedures, and Additional Services. Accreditation must be renewed every three years. The National Association of Professional Pet Sitters offers the certified pet sitter designation to applicants who complete a home-study course and pass an online examination. Certification tells prospective clients that you have met industry standards, and may increase your chances of being hired.

Michele Finley has a different view on certification. "I really don't think such things are necessary," she says. "All you need to know can be learned by working for a good sitter and reading pet health and behavioral newsletters."

Though there is no particular pet sitting license required of pet sitters, insurance protection is important. Liability insurance protects the pet sitter from lawsuits; both the NAPPS and PSI offer group liability packages to its members. Pet sitters must also be bonded.

Bonding assures the pet owners that if anything is missing from their homes after a pet sitting appointment, they can receive compensation immediately.

Other Requirements
You must love animals and animals must love you. But this love for animals can't be your only motivation—keep in mind that, as a pet sitter, you will be in business for yourself. You will not have a boss to give you assignments, and you won't have a secretary or book-keeper to do the paperwork. You also won't have employees to take over on weekends, holidays, and days when you are not feeling well. Though some pet sitters are successful enough to afford assistance, most must handle all the aspects of their businesses by themselves. So, you should be self-motivated, and as dedicated to the management of your business as you are to the animals.

Pet owners entrust you with the care of their pets and their homes, so you must be trustworthy and reliable. You should also be organized and prepared for emergency situations. And not only must you be patient with the pets and their owners, but also with the development of your business: it will take a few years to build up a good list of clients.

As a pet sitter, you must also be ready for the dirty work—you'll be cleaning litter boxes and animal messes within the house. On dog walks, you will be picking up after them on the street. You may be giving animals medications. You'll also be cleaning aquariums and birdcages.

"Work for an established pet sitter to see how you like it," Finley advises. "It's a very physically demanding job and not many can stand it for long on a full-time basis." Pet sitting isn't for those who just want a nine-to-five desk job. Your day will be spent moving from house to house, taking animals into backyards, and walking dogs around the neighborhoods. Though you may be able to develop a set schedule for yourself, you really will have to arrange your work hours around the hours of your clients. Some pet sitters start in the early morning hours, while others only work afternoons or evenings. To stay in business, a pet sitter must be prepared to work weekends, holidays, and long hours in the summertime.

EXPLORING

There are many books, newsletters, and magazines devoted to pet care. *Pet Sitting for Profit,* by Patti Moran (Howell Book House, 2006) is just one of many books that can offer insight into pet sitting as a career. Magazines such as *Pet Sitter's WORLD* (http://www. petsit.com/media/publication_professional.php) can also teach you about the requirements of professional animal care. And many books discuss the ins and outs of small business ownership.

Try pet sitting for a neighbor or family member to get a sense of the responsibilities of the job. Some pet sitters hire assistants on an independent contractor basis; contact an area pet sitter listed in the phone book or with one of the professional organizations, and see if you can "hire on" for a day or two. Not only will you learn firsthand the duties of a pet sitter, but you'll also see how the business is run.

EMPLOYERS

Nearly all pet sitters are self-employed, although a few may work for other successful pet sitters who have built up a large enough clientele to require help. It takes most pet sitters an appreciable period of time to build up a business substantial enough to make a living without other means of income. However, the outlook for this field is excellent and start-up costs are minimal, making it a good choice for animal lovers who want to work for themselves. For those who have good business sense and a great deal of ambition, the potential for success is good.

STARTING OUT

You're not likely to find job listings under "pet sitter" in the newspaper. Most pet sitters schedule all their work themselves. However, you may find ads in the classifieds or in weekly community papers from pet owners looking to hire pet sitters. Some people who become pet sitters have backgrounds in animal care—they may have worked for vets, breeders, or pet shops. These people enter the business with a client list already in hand, having made contacts with many pet owners. But, if you are just starting out in animal care, you need to develop a list of references. This may mean volunteering your time to friends and neighbors, or working very cheaply. If you're willing to actually stay in the house while the pet owners are on vacation, you should be able to find plenty of pet sitting opportunities in the summertime. Post your name, phone number, and availability on the bulletin boards of grocery stores, colleges, and coffee shops around town. Once you've developed a list of references, and have made connections with pet owners, you can start expanding, and increasing your profits.

Susan Clark runs a professional dog-walking business in Brooklyn, New York. She suggests another way of breaking into the business. "I started my business," she says, "by visiting pet stores and asking if they would supply me with their mailing lists; in return, when I went door to door with my own postcards I would include their business cards. Many pet store owners were kind enough to agree to this arrangement. I have to say, though, [that] the majority of my business came from two other sources: word of mouth and referrals from other dog walkers in the neighborhood. I knew a great deal of dog owners in the area because I would go to the dog runs with my own two dogs. The minute I mentioned I was thinking about opening up a dog-walking service, I was in business. My dog walker and boarder were incredibly supportive and also sent business my way. I was very fortunate, and have never forgotten their generosity so I do the same for other new dog walkers in the neighborhood."

ADVANCEMENT

Your advancement will be a result of your own hard work; the more time you dedicate to your business, the bigger the business will become. The success of any small business can be very unpredictable. For some, a business can build very quickly, for others it may take years. Some pet sitters start out part time, perhaps even volunteering, then may find themselves with enough business to quit their full-time jobs and devote themselves entirely to pet sitting. Once your business takes off, you may be able to afford an assistant, or an entire staff. Some pet sitters even have franchises across the country. You may even choose to develop your business into a much larger operation, such as a dog day care facility.

EARNINGS

Pet sitters set their own prices, charging by the visit, the hour, or the week. They may also charge consultation fees, and additional fees on holidays. They may have special pricing plans in place, such as for emergency situations or for administering medications. Depending on the kinds of animals (sometimes pet sitters charge less to care for cats than dogs), pet sitters generally charge between $8 and $20 for a 30-minute visit. The average per-visit rate for dog walking was $18.08 in 2008, according to Pet Sitters International (PSI). Pet sitters charged $19.86 for a 33-minute visit caring for pets with special needs. PSI conducted a survey of annual salaries and discovered that the median revenue is $20,000. Some very successful pet sitters have annual salaries of more than $100,000, while others only make $5,000 a year. Though a pet sitter can make a good profit in any area of the country, a bigger city will offer more clients. Pet sitters in their first five years of business are unlikely to make more than $10,000 a year; pet sitters who have had businesses for eight years or more may earn more than $40,000 a year.

Pet sitters who work full time for a company usually receive benefits such as health and life insurance, sick leave, vacation days, and a savings and pension plan. Self-employed pet sitters must provide their own benefits.

WORK ENVIRONMENT

Some pet sitters prefer to work close to their homes; Michele Finley only walks dogs in her Brooklyn neighborhood. In a smaller town, however, pet sitters have to do a fair amount of driving from place to place. Depending on the needs of the animals, the pet sitter will let the pets outside for play and exercise. Although filling food and water bowls and performing other chores within the house is generally peaceful work, walking dogs on busy city sidewalks can be stressful. And in the wintertime, you'll spend a fair amount of time out in the inclement weather. "Icy streets are murder," Finley says. "And I don't like dealing with people who hate dogs and are always yelling to get the dog away from them."

Though you will have some initial interaction with pet owners when getting house keys, taking down phone numbers, and meeting the pets and learning about their needs, most of your work will be alone with the animals. But you will not be totally isolated; if dog walking in the city, you will meet other dog owners and other people in the neighborhood.

OUTLOOK

Pet sitting as a small business is expected to skyrocket in the coming years. Most pet sitters charge fees comparable to kennels and boarders, but some charge less. And many pet owners prefer to leave their pets in the house, rather than take the pets to unfamiliar locations. This has made pet sitting a desirable and cost-effective alternative to other pet care situations. Pet sitters have been successful in cities both large and small. In the last few years, pet sitting has been featured in the *Wall Street Journal* and other national publications.

Woman's Day magazine listed pet sitting as one of the top-grossing businesses for women.

Because a pet sitting business requires little money to start up, many more people may enter the business hoping to make a tidy profit. This could lead to heavier competition; it could also hurt the reputation of pet sitting if too many irresponsible and unprepared people run bad businesses. But if pet owners remain cautious when hiring pet sitters, the unreliable workers will have trouble maintaining clients.

FOR MORE INFORMATION

For information about pet care, contact
American Society for the Prevention of Cruelty to Animals
424 East 92nd Street
New York, NY 10128-6804
Tel: 212-876-7700
http://www.aspca.org

The association offers membership options for walkers, groomers, kennel owners, veterinarians, pet sitters, and other professionals in the dog world—including a membership category for those who have "an active interest in making a career within the canine profession, but do not yet have the experience to qualify for acceptance" at professional membership levels. Visit its Web site for information on membership, training, and other topics.
International Association of Canine Professionals
Tel: 407-469-2008
E-mail: iacpadmin@mindspring.com
http://canineprofessionals.com

For information on pet setting and certification, contact
National Association of Professional Pet Sitters
15000 Commerce Parkway, Suite C
Mt. Laurel, NJ 08054-2212
Tel: 856-439-0324
E-mail: NAPPS@ahint.com
http://www.petsitters.org

This is a professional membership association for pet boarders, sitters, groomers, animal trainers, and pet suppliers. It offers a membership category for any "individual who is interested in the pet care industry, but who does not presently operate a non-veterinary pet care business." Visit the association's Web site for information on training opportunities, membership, networking events, and pet health.

Pet Care Services Association
401 North Michigan Avenue, Suite 2200
Chicago, IL 60611-4245
Tel: 800-218-9123
http://www.petcareservices.org

For certification, careers, and small business information, as well as general information about pet sitting, contact

Pet Sitters International
201 East King Street
King, NC 27021-9161
Tel: 336-983-9222
http://www.petsit.com

——— INTERVIEW ———

Jill Nuciolo is the owner of FluffyPaw's Pet Luv, a pet sitting service in New York. She discussed her career with the editors of Careers in Focus: Animal Care.

Q. Can you tell us a little about your business? Why did you decide to enter this career?

A. I started FluffyPaw's Pet Luv in 1995. I looked in the yellow pages and there seemed to be a lot of pet sitters so actually I started out advertising to transport, medicate, and walk pets. Pet sitting was in there, but not a top priority. It turns out I didn't realize that pet sitters stayed within a certain distance and none of the ones listed would come to the town I was in. Before I knew it I was swamped. Within a few months, I no longer offered any of the other services except the walking and medicating. I was the only one servicing my area for a few years. I had been an office manager for 17 years when I decided to finally do something with animals. It had always been my dream and goal to spend my days doing something to help animals.

Q. What are your main and secondary job duties?

A. Pet sitting is my main job duty, which includes all the care the pet needs. This also includes bringing in paper and mail, watering plants, turning lights on/off, etc. Midday walks are short trips to let the dog out in the yard to play or take them for a walk. I also will make trips to houses to administer medication only, if the owner finds it difficult to do. There is also office work—invoicing, returning calls, following through with mailings to remind people you are still in business.

Q. What are some of the pros and cons of your career?

A. Pros: Nothing compares to those happy furry faces when you walk in the door! When you've been making many trips to a house with a very shy cat that you never see except with the flashlight under the bed and then one day the cats walks right up to get petted. I had to be careful to control my excitement because if I scared the poor cat I would have had to start from the beginning! Another pro is being able to decide your own workload—how busy you want to be.

Cons: You pretty much work 365 days a year. Plan on working holidays. People will call last minute so your plans get canceled. When you first start out you better plan on all that or you won't be getting customers.

Q. What are the most important personal and professional qualities for pet sitters?

A. Without a doubt—honesty. If you can't prove yourself to be 100 percent honest, you won't be in business long. You are going into people's homes while they are away and they need to feel comfortable with you doing that.

An absolute love and devotion to animals. This is one profession that you have to love animals or you will burn out very fast. All my animals become dear to me, and I probably become more protective of them than their owners! I say that because they are already missing their owners so I don't want to do anything that adds any more stress to them. It's not easy to go out in the evening to work more when you've put in a whole day already. And if you live where it snows—there is nothing harder than bundling up and heading out in that snowstorm. But the animals need and depend on you and the only thing that gets me out in those conditions is knowing that there is a wonderful dog or cat waiting.

Punctuality. Even though no one is there you need to be on time to get the dogs outside to relieve themselves, give medications, and because it's part of the honesty quality. Believe me— neighbors watch! They know when you get there, they know how long you stay, and they tell your customer.

Patience. You are dealing with animals—expect anything. No two visits are ever alike!

Sense of humor. If you can't laugh through these surprises, laugh even though you walked into a mess that was made, or, most important, laugh at yourself then you will have a hard time doing this. You need to not take the actions that are not in your control too seriously. You can't dwell on things. You have to laugh and put it in its place, learn from it, and move on.

Q. What is one of the most interesting or rewarding things that happened to you while working in this field?

A. There are many rewards to the field—including the love from the animals. The reward of the customer being satisfied and hiring you again. I like knowing I made a difference. I like to make people happy so when I can do something above and beyond with a successful outcome that is highly rewarding to me. I like knowing people can go away and not worry about their homes and pets because of the impact I made with their pets.

Veterinarians

OVERVIEW

The *veterinarian,* or *doctor of veterinary medicine,* diagnoses and controls animal diseases, treats sick and injured animals medically and surgically, prevents transmission of animal diseases, and advises owners on proper care of pets and livestock. Veterinarians are dedicated to the protection of the health and welfare of all animals and to society as a whole. There are about 59,700 veterinarians in the United States.

HISTORY

The first school of veterinary medicine was opened in 1762 at Lyons, France. Nearly 100 years later, a French physician and veterinarian named Alexandre Francois Liautard immigrated to the United States and became a leader in the movement to establish veterinary medicine as a science. Through his efforts, an organization was started in 1863 that later became the American Veterinary Medical Association. Veterinary medicine has made great strides since its introduction in this country, one advance being the significant reduction in animal diseases contracted by humans.

QUICK FACTS

School Subjects
Biology
Chemistry

Personal Skills
Helping/teaching
Technical/scientific

Work Environment
Primarily indoors
Primarily one location

Minimum Education Level
Medical degree

Salary Range
$41,636 to $80,510 to
$142,910+

Certification or Licensing
Required

Outlook
Much faster than the average

DOT
073

GOE
03.02.01

NOC
3114

O*NET-SOC
29-1131.00

THE JOB

Veterinarians care for pets—large and small. They ensure a safe food supply by maintaining the health of food animals. They also protect the public from residues of herbicides, pesticides, and antibiotics in food. Veterinarians may be involved in wildlife preservation and conservation and use their knowledge to increase food production through genetics, animal feed production, and preventive medicine.

Learn More About It

McBride, Douglas F., and Miriam and Harvey Austrin. *Learning Veterinary Terminology.* 2d ed. St. Louis: Mosby, 2001.
Robinson, Phillip T. *Life at the Zoo: Behind the Scenes with the Animal Doctors.* New York: Columbia University Press, 2007.
Spelman, Lucy H., and Ted Y. Mashima. *The Rhino with Glue-On Shoes: And Other Surprising True Stories of Zoo Vets and Their Patients.* New York: Delacorte Press, 2008.
Stewart, Liz. *Vault Career Guide to Veterinary and Animal Careers.* New York: Vault Inc., 2008.
Trout, Nick. *Tell Me Where It Hurts: A Day of Humor, Healing and Hope in My Life as an Animal Surgeon.* New York: Broadway Books, 2009.
Wells, Jeff. *All My Patients Have Tales: Favorite Stories from a Vet's Practice.* New York: St. Martin's Press, 2009.

About 80 percent of veterinarians are employed in solo or group veterinary medicine practices. Although some veterinarians treat all kinds of animals, more than half limit their practice to companion animals such as dogs, cats, and birds. A smaller number of veterinarians work mainly with horses, cattle, pigs, sheep, goats, and poultry. Today, a veterinarian may treat llamas, catfish, or ostriches as well. Others are employed by wildlife management groups, zoos, aquariums, ranches, feedlots, fish farms, and animal shelters.

Veterinarians in private practice diagnose and treat animal health problems. During yearly checkups, the veterinarian records the animal's temperature and weight; inspects its mouth, eyes, and ears; examines the skin or coat for any signs of abnormalities; observes any peculiarities in the animal's behavior; and discusses the animals eating, sleeping, and exercise habits at length with the owner. The veterinarian will also check the animal's vaccination records and administer inoculations for rabies, distemper, and other diseases if necessary. If the veterinarian or owner notes any special concerns, or if the animal is taken to the veterinarian for a specific procedure, such as spaying or neutering, dental cleaning, or setting broken bones, the animal may stay at the veterinarian's office for one or several days for surgery, observation, or extended treatments. If a sick or wounded animal is beyond medical help, the veterinarian may, with the consent of the owner, have to euthanize the animal.

Veterinarians in private clinical practice become specialists in surgery, anesthesiology, dentistry, internal medicine, ophthalmology, or radiology. Many veterinarians also pursue advanced degrees in the basic sciences, such as anatomy, microbiology, and physiology. Veterinarians who seek specialty board certification in one of 20 specialty fields must complete a two- to five-year residency program and must pass an additional examination. Some veterinarians combine their degree in veterinary medicine with a degree in business (M.B.A.) or law (J.D.).

During office visits and surgery, veterinarians use traditional medical instruments, such as stethoscopes, thermometers, and surgical instruments, and standard tests, such as X-rays and diagnostic medical sonography, to evaluate the animal's health. Veterinarians may also prescribe drugs for the animal, which the owner purchases at the veterinarian's office.

Some veterinarians work in public and corporate sectors. Many are employed by city, county, state, provincial, or federal government agencies that investigate, test for, and control diseases in companion animals, livestock, and poultry that affect both animal and human health. Veterinarians also play an important public health role. For example, veterinarians played an important part in conquering diseases such as malaria and yellow fever.

Pharmaceutical and biomedical research firms hire veterinarians to develop, test, and supervise the production of drugs, chemicals, and biological products such as antibiotics and vaccines that are designed for human and animal use. Some veterinarians are employed in management, technical sales and services, and marketing in agribusiness, pet food companies, and pharmaceutical companies. Still other veterinarians are engaged in research and teaching at veterinary medical schools, working with racetracks or animal-related enterprises, or working within the military, public health corps, and space agencies.

The U.S. Department of Agriculture has opportunities for veterinarians in the Food Safety and Inspection Service and the Animal and Plant Health Inspection Service, notably in the areas of food hygiene and safety, animal welfare, animal disease control, and research. Veterinarians also are employed by the Environmental Protection Agency to deal with public health and environmental risks to the human population.

Veterinarians are often assisted by *veterinary technicians* and *technologists,* who may conduct basic tests, record an animal's medical history for the veterinarian's review, and assist the veterinarian in surgical procedures.

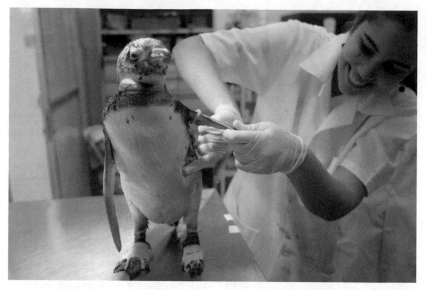

A penguin, rescued off the coast of Rio de Janeiro, Brazil, receives treatment from a veterinarian. *(Ricardo Moraes, AP Photo)*

REQUIREMENTS

High School

For the high school student who is interested in admission to a school of veterinary medicine, a college preparatory course is a wise choice. A strong emphasis on science classes such as biology, chemistry, and anatomy is highly recommended.

Postsecondary Training

The doctor of veterinary medicine (D.V.M.) degree requires a minimum of four years of study at an accredited college of veterinary medicine. Although many of these colleges do not require a bachelor's degree for admission, most require applicants to have completed 45 to 90 hours of undergraduate study. It is possible to obtain preveterinary training at a junior college, but since admission to colleges of veterinary medicine is an extremely competitive process, most students receive degrees from four-year colleges before applying. In addition to academic instruction, veterinary education includes clinical experience in diagnosing disease and treating animals, performing surgery, and performing laboratory work in anatomy, biochemistry, and other scientific and medical subjects.

There are 28 colleges of veterinary medicine in the United States that are accredited by the Council on Education of the American Veterinary Medical Association (AVMA). Each college of veterinary medicine has its own preveterinary requirements, which typically include basic language arts, social sciences, humanities, mathematics, chemistry, and biological and physical sciences. Veterinarians in private clinical practice become specialists in surgery, anesthesiology, dentistry, internal medicine, ophthalmology, or radiology. Many veterinarians also pursue advanced degrees in the basic sciences, such as anatomy, microbiology, and physiology.

Applicants to schools of veterinary medicine usually must have grades of "B" or better, especially in the sciences. Applicants must take the Veterinary College Admission Test, Medical College Admission Test, or the Graduate Record Examination. Only about one-third of applicants to schools of veterinary medicine are admitted, due to small class sizes and limited facilities. Most colleges give preference to candidates with animal- or veterinary-related experience. Colleges usually give preference to in-state applicants because most colleges of veterinary medicine are state-supported. There are regional agreements in which states without veterinary schools send students to designated regional schools.

Veterinary medicine students typically participate in one or more internships during their college careers. The internships allow them to learn more about career options in the field and make valuable industry contacts.

Certification or Licensing

Veterinarians who seek specialty board certification in one of nearly 40 specialty fields must complete a two- to five-year residency program and pass an additional examination. Some veterinarians combine their degree in veterinary medicine with a degree in business or law. Contact the AVMA American Board of Veterinary Specialties (http://www.avma.org/education/abvs) for more information.

All states and the District of Columbia require that veterinarians be licensed to practice private clinical medicine. To obtain a license, applicants must have a D.V.M. degree from an accredited or approved college of veterinary medicine. They must also pass one or more national examinations and an examination in the state in which they plan to practice.

Few states issue licenses to veterinarians already licensed by another state. Thus, if a veterinarian moves from one state to another, he or she will probably have to go through the licensing process again. Nearly all states require veterinarians to attend continuing education courses in order to maintain their licenses. Veterinarians may be employed by a government agency (such as the U.S. Department of Agriculture) or by some academic institutions without having a state license.

Other Requirements

Individuals who are interested in veterinary medicine should have an inquiring mind and keen powers of observation. Aptitude and interest in the biological sciences are important. Veterinarians need a lifelong interest in scientific learning as well as a liking and understanding of animals. Veterinarians should be able to meet, talk, and work well with a variety of people. An ability to communicate with the animal owner is as important in a veterinarian as diagnostic skills.

Veterinarians use state-of-the-art medical equipment, such as electron microscopes, laser surgery, radiation therapy, and ultrasound, to diagnose animal diseases and to treat sick or injured animals. Although manual dexterity and physical stamina are often required, especially for farm vets, important roles in veterinary medicine can be adapted for those with disabilities.

Interaction with animal owners is a very important part of being a veterinarian. The discussions between vet and owner are critical to the veterinarian's diagnosis, so he or she must be able to communicate effectively and get along with a wide variety of personalities. Veterinarians may have to euthanize (that is, humanely kill) an animal that is very sick or severely injured and cannot get well. When a beloved pet dies, the veterinarian must deal with the owner's grief and loss.

EXPLORING

High school students interested in becoming veterinarians may find part time or volunteer work on farms, in small-animal clinics, or in pet shops, animal shelters, or research laboratories. Participation in extracurricular activities such as 4-H are good ways to learn about the care of animals. Such experience is important because, as already noted, many schools of veterinary medicine have established experience with animals as a criterion for admission to their programs. Other methods of exploration include talking to a veterinarian about his or her career, reading books and magazines about veterinary science, and visiting the Web sites of veterinary associations and veterinary medical colleges.

EMPLOYERS

Approximately 59,700 veterinarians are employed in the United States. Veterinarians may work for schools and universities, wildlife management groups, zoos, aquariums, ranches, feed lots, fish farms, pet food or pharmaceutical companies, and the government (mainly in the U.S. Departments of Agriculture and the U.S. Food and Drug Administration's Center for Veterinary Medicine, but also for the Department of Homeland Security). The vast majority, however, are employed by veterinary clinical practices or hospitals. Many successful veterinarians in private practice are self-employed and may even employ other veterinarians. An increase in the demand for veterinarians is anticipated, particularly for those who specialize in areas related to public health issues such as food safety and disease control. Cities and large metropolitan areas will probably provide the bulk of new jobs for these specialists, while jobs for veterinarians who specialize in large animals will be focused in remote, rural areas.

STARTING OUT

The only way to become a veterinarian is through the prescribed degree program, and vet schools are set up to assist their graduates in finding employment. Veterinarians who wish to enter private clinical practice must have a license to practice in their particular state before opening an office. Licenses are obtained by passing the state's examination.

Information about employment opportunities can be obtained by contacting employers directly or through career services offices of veterinary medicine colleges. Additionally, professional associations such as the American Association of Zoo Veterinarians, the American Association of Wildlife Veterinarians, the Association of American Veterinary Medical Colleges, and the American Veterinary Medical Association offer job listings at their Web sites.

ADVANCEMENT

New graduate veterinarians may enter private clinical practice, usually as employees in an established practice, or become employees of the U.S. government as meat and poultry inspectors, disease control workers, and commissioned officers in the U.S. Public Health Service or the military. New graduates may also enter internships and residencies at veterinary colleges and large private and public veterinary practices or become employed by industrial firms.

The veterinarian who is employed by a government agency may advance in grade and salary after accumulating time and experience on the job. For the veterinarian in private clinical practice, advancement usually consists of an expanding practice and the higher income that will result from it or becoming an owner of several practices.

Those who teach or do research may obtain a doctorate and move from the rank of instructor to that of full professor, or they may advance to an administrative position.

EARNINGS

The U.S. Department of Labor (DOL) reports that median annual earnings of veterinarians were $80,510 in 2009. Salaries ranged from less than $47,670 to more than $142,910. The mean annual salary for veterinarians working for the federal government was $84,200 in 2009.

The average starting salary for veterinary medical college graduates who worked exclusively with small animals was $64,744 in 2008, according to a survey by the American Veterinary Medical Association. Those who worked exclusively with large animals earned an average of $62,424. Equine veterinarians earned an average of $41,636 to start. The average starting salary for all veterinarians was $48,328.

Benefits include paid vacation, health, disability, life insurance, and retirement or pension plans. Self-employed veterinarians must provide their own benefits.

WORK ENVIRONMENT

Veterinarians usually treat companion and food animals in hospitals and clinics. Those in large animal practice also work out of well-equipped trucks or cars and may drive considerable distances to farms and ranches. They may work outdoors in all kinds of weather. The chief risk for veterinarians is injury by animals; however, modern tranquilizers and technology have made it much easier to work on all types of animals.

Most veterinarians work long hours, often 50 or more hours a week. Although those in private clinical practice may work nights and weekends, the increased number of emergency clinics has reduced the amount of time private practitioners have to be on call. Large animal practitioners tend to work more irregular hours than those in small animal practice, industry, or government. Veterinarians who are just starting a practice tend to work longer hours.

OUTLOOK

Employment of veterinarians is expected to grow much faster than the average for all careers through 2018, according to the DOL. The number of pets (especially cats) is expected to increase because of rising incomes and an increase in the number of people aged 34 to 59, among whom pet ownership has historically been the highest. Approximately 62 percent of U.S. households owned a pet in 2009, according to the American Pet Products Association. Many single adults and senior citizens have come to appreciate animal ownership. Pet owners also may be willing to pay for more elective and intensive care than in the past. In addition, emphasis on scientific methods of breeding and raising livestock, poultry, and fish and continued support for public health and disease control programs will contribute to the demand for veterinarians.

The outlook is good for veterinarians with specialty training. Demand for specialists in toxicology, laboratory animal medicine, and pathology is expected to increase. Most jobs for specialists will be in metropolitan areas. Prospects for veterinarians who concentrate on environmental and public health issues, aquaculture, and food animal practice appear to be excellent because of perceived increased need in these areas. Positions in small animal specialties will be competitive. Opportunities in farm animal specialties will be excellent since most of these positions are located in remote, rural areas, where many veterinarians do not want to practice.

FOR MORE INFORMATION

For career information, contact
Academy of Rural Veterinarians
1450 Western Avenue, Suite 101
Albany, NY 12203-3539
Tel: 518-694-0056
E-mail: arv@caphill.com
http://www.ruralvets.com

The association represents the professional interests of veterinarians who primarily treat companion animals. Visit its Web site for information on practice issues and publications.
American Animal Hospital Association
12575 West Bayaud Avenue
Lakewood, CO 80228-2021
Tel: 303-986-2800
E-mail: info@aahanet.org
http://www.aahanet.org

For information on equine veterinary science, contact
American Association of Equine Practitioners
4075 Iron Works Parkway
Lexington, KY 40511-8483
Tel: 859-233-0147
E-mail: aaepoffice@aaep.org
http://www.aaep.org

Visit the association's Web site for job listings and information about wildlife veterinarians.
American Association of Wildlife Veterinarians
http://www.aawv.net

Visit the association's Web site for job listings, news about zoos around the world, the Journal of Zoo & Wildlife Medicine, *information on internships and externships and zoo and wildlife clubs for veterinary students, and discussion boards.*
American Association of Zoo Veterinarians
581705 White Oak Road
Yulee, FL 32097-2169
Tel: 904-225-3275
http://www.aazv.org

For information on animal behavior, contact
American College of Veterinary Behaviorists
http://www.dacvb.org

For more information on careers, schools, and resources, contact
American Veterinary Medical Association
1931 North Meacham Road, Suite 100
Schaumburg, IL 60173-4360
Tel: 800-248-2862
E-mail: avmainfo@avma.org
http://www.avma.org

For information on veterinary opportunities in the federal government, contact
Animal and Plant Health Inspection Service
1400 Independence Avenue, SW
Washington, DC 20250-0002
E-mail: APHIS.Web@aphis.usda.gov
http://www.aphis.usda.gov

For information educational programs, contact
Association of American Veterinary Medical Colleges
1101 Vermont Avenue, NW, Suite 301
Washington, DC 20005-3539
Tel: 202-371-9195
http://www.aavmc.org

For career information, contact
Association of Exotic Mammal Veterinarians
PO Box 396
Weare, NH 03281-0396
E-mail: info@aemv.org
http://www.aemv.org

For information on education and internships, contact
International Association for Aquatic Animal Medicine
E-mail: admin@iaaam.org
http://www.iaaam.org

The association offers membership options for walkers, groomers, kennel owners, veterinarians, pet sitters, and other professionals in the dog world—including a membership category for those who have "an active interest in making a career within the canine profession, but do not yet have the experience to qualify for acceptance" at professional membership levels. Visit its Web site for information on membership, training, and other topics.
International Association of Canine Professionals
Tel: 407-469-2008
E-mail: iacpadmin@mindspring.com
http://canineprofessionals.com

For information on veterinary careers in Canada, contact
Canadian Veterinary Medical Association
339 Booth Street
Ottawa, ON K1R 7K1 Canada
Tel: 613-236-1162
E-mail: admin@cvma-acmv.org
http://www.canadianveterinarians.net

INTERVIEW

Dr. Randy Wheeler is the assistant state veterinarian for the Iowa Department of Agriculture and Land Stewardship (IDALS). He discussed his career with the editors of Careers in Focus: Animal Care.

Q. Can you please tell us a little about yourself?

A. I grew up on a family "century farm" (a farm that has been in the family for at least 100 years) in Madison County, Iowa, and received my doctorate of veterinary medicine (D.V.M.) from Iowa State in 1977.

I have been associated with veterinary medicine for more than 35 years in a number of venues. As an undergrad and during my four years in veterinary school, I was an animal caretaker and later a lab technician at the Iowa State Veterinary Medical Research Institute. My first three years of private practice were served in a predominantly small animal and equine Des Moines-based veterinary clinic, which included work at the Des Moines Blank Park Zoo.

I attained my original career goal to practice in my hometown and for the next 27 years I was a partner in a multiple-person mixed animal practice in Winterset, Iowa (the birthplace of John Wayne and myself!).

The last three years I have worked in the public veterinary arena at the Animal Industry Bureau of the Department of Agriculture in Des Moines, where I am the assistant state veterinarian and Iowa Veterinary Rapid Response Team coordinator.

Q. Why did you decide to enter this career?

A. My heritage was in animal husbandry and agriculture, and I was very interested in science and medicine and all types of animals. Our farm had everything from dairy and beef cattle to hogs, horses, and hens—so animals and their care were a big part of my upbringing. It was almost preordained that I would do something with animals and being a veterinarian was my lifelong aspiration, in part due to my love for animals and their care. I admired the profession and how it was perceived by the public.

Q. What are your main and secondary job duties?

A. As assistant state veterinarian, under the direction of the state veterinarian, I am tasked with the oversight of animal welfare and animal disease programs. I am supervisor to the five IDALS livestock inspectors and animal health technicians who deal with the licensure and inspection of more than 1,500 animal care facilities including kennels, pet stores, commercial breeders, pounds and shelters, livestock markets and dealers, and hatcheries.

I work with four state district veterinarians who deal with the various state and federal disease programs such as tuberculosis and brucellosis, Johne's disease, scrapie and chronic wasting disease, and pseudorabies to name a few. And I assist the state veterinarian in matters concerning animal disease, animal importation, and health requirements and rules for exhibitions such as county fairs and the Iowa State Fair. My secondary role is serving as the director of the IDALS animal emergency response task force called the Iowa Veterinary Rapid Response Team (IVRRT), which is comprised of more than 400 veterinarians, veterinary technicians, industry representatives, veterinary students, and producers who are a voluntary group who receive training in emergency animal disease response and disaster management. The IVRRT group was instrumental in the support and success in dealing with animal welfare issues during the winter storms of 2007/2008 and the 2008 flood and tornado situations.

Q. What are the primary animals for which IDALS is responsible?

A. Companion animals and livestock, including poultry and farmed deer and elk, that are involved in inter- and intrastate commerce. All animals covered by state law and statutes are covered by the Animal Industry Bureau of the Department of Agriculture.

Q. What are the most important personal and professional qualities for veterinarians?

A. There are many admirable qualities that all professionals should maintain, but two of the more important I believe are integrity and compassion, but I would be remiss if I didn't mention common sense. Having a DVM carries along with it a long-standing tradition of care and understanding and professionalism in dealing with the well-being of animals.

Q. What advice would you give to high school students who are interested in becoming veterinarians?

A. Be committed and persevere. It will take hard work and devotion to attain a degree in veterinary medicine.

Be passionate and caring. It is a wonderful profession deserving of talented individuals who care about the animal industry.

Be forewarned and aware. It is a "people business," not just about animals! Most of the animals you will be involved with will have owners to deal with. It will serve you well to learn social skills, as well as scientific skills, to get the most out of this profession. Veterinary medicine is one of the most rewarding and interesting professions I can think of.

Q. What is the future employment outlook for your field?

A. A shortage of veterinarians is already being seen, especially in the large animal and regulatory/public sectors.

The venues are numerous including military, academia, research, public health, regulatory/governmental, industry, nutritional, and, of course, private practice. But you can specialize in many fields—from animal species to surgical specialties, to holistic and alternative medical fields. The profession has many faces and opportunities.

Q. What is one of the most interesting or rewarding things that happened to you while working in this field?

A. The relationships you develop with the state animal officials of the other 49 states and the travel and meetings are both rewarding and very interesting. There is a challenge and responsibility associated with safeguarding our state's and the nation's animal industry, which can be daunting at times but very stimulating, too. I loved my 30 years in private practice. It never entered my mind to work in the governmental/public practice arena of veterinary medicine, but it has been a great experience in my veterinary career. As I mentioned earlier, there are many various job opportunities in the field of veterinary medicine and each has its own rewards and benefits, so I would encourage all who are interested in being a veterinarian to survey these venues—the diversity of the profession might surprise many people.

In regards to one specific incident I have been associated with as assistant state vet and IVRRT coordinator, the Parkersburg tornado and the 2008 flood situations had to be two of the more interesting scenarios. The response from the Department of Agriculture, the IVRRT volunteers, and the scope of involvement with local, state, industry, and federal government was overwhelming. The collaboration and cooperation of so many individuals and agencies, such as Animal Rescue League and the many other animal welfare organizations, and various entities, including USDA Veterinary Services and Kirkwood Community College, was an experience that is hard to explain. The heartwarming and heartbreaking stories were many, but the overall outcome was a truly memorable success in dealing with the human and animal spirit.

Veterinary Technicians

OVERVIEW

Veterinary technicians provide support and assistance to veterinarians. They work in a variety of environments, including zoos, animal hospitals, clinics, private practices, kennels, and laboratories. Work may involve large or small animals or both. Although most veterinary technicians work with domestic animals, some professional settings may require treating exotic or endangered species. There are approximately 79,600 veterinary technicians and technologists employed in the United States.

HISTORY

As the scope of veterinary practices grew and developed, veterinarians began to need assistants. At first the role was informal, with veterinary assistants being trained by the doctors they worked for. However, in the latter half of the 20th century, the education, and thus the profession, of veterinary assistants became formalized. They are now an indispensable part of a veterinary practice.

THE JOB

Many pet owners depend on veterinarians to maintain the health and well-being of their pets. Veterinary clinics and private practices are the primary settings for animal care. In assisting veterinarians, veterinary technicians play an integral role in the care of animals within this particular environment.

A veterinary technician is the person who performs much of the laboratory testing procedures commonly associated with veterinary care. In fact, approximately 50 percent of a veterinary technician's

A veterinary technician hand-feeds a rescued seal pup at the Vancouver Aquarium's Marine Mammal Rescue Center in Vancouver, Canada. *(Darryl Dyck, AP Photo/The Canadian Press)*

duties involve laboratory testing. Laboratory assignments usually include taking and developing X-rays, performing parasitology tests, and examining various samples taken from the animal's body, such as blood and stool. A veterinary technician may also assist the veterinarian with necropsies in an effort to determine the cause of an animal's death.

In a clinic or private practice, a veterinary technician assists the veterinarian with surgical procedures. This generally entails preparing the animal for surgery by shaving the incision area and applying a topical antibacterial agent. Surgical anesthesia is administered and controlled by the veterinary technician. Throughout the surgical process, the technician tracks the surgical instruments and monitors the animal's vital signs. If an animal is very ill and has no chance for survival, or an overcrowded animal shelter is unable to find a home for a donated or stray animal, the veterinary technician may be required to assist in euthanizing it.

During routine examinations and checkups, veterinary technicians will help restrain the animals. They may perform ear cleaning and nail clipping procedures as part of regular animal care. Outside the examination and surgery rooms, veterinary technicians perform additional duties. In most settings, they record, replenish, and maintain pharmaceutical equipment and other supplies.

Veterinary technicians also may work in a zoo. Here, job duties, such as laboratory testing, are quite similar, but practices are more specialized. Unlike in private practice, the *zoo veterinary technician* is not required to explain treatment to pet owners; however, he or she may have to discuss an animal's treatment or progress with zoo veterinarians, zoo curators, and other zoo professionals. A zoo veterinary technician's work also may differ from private practice in that it may be necessary for the technician to observe the animal in its habitat, which could require working outdoors. Additionally, zoo veterinary technicians usually work with exotic or endangered species. This is a very competitive and highly desired area of practice in the veterinary technician field. There are only a few zoos in each state; thus, a limited number of job opportunities exist within these zoos. To break into this area of practice, veterinary technicians must be among the best in the field.

Veterinary technicians also work in research. Most research opportunities for veterinary technicians are in academic environments with veterinary medicine or medical science programs. Again, laboratory testing may account for many of the duties; however, the veterinary technicians participate in very important animal research projects from start to finish.

Technicians are also needed in rural areas. Farmers require veterinary services for the care of farm animals such as pigs, cows, horses, dogs, cats, sheep, mules, and chickens. It is often essential for the veterinarian and technician to drive to the farmer's residence because animals are usually treated on-site.

Another area in which veterinary technicians work is that of animal training, such as at an obedience school or with show business animals being trained for the circus or movies. Veterinary technicians may also be employed in information systems technology, where information on animals is compiled and provided to the public via the Internet.

No matter what the setting, a veterinary technician must be an effective communicator and proficient in basic computer applications. In clinical or private practice, it is usually the veterinary technician who conveys and explains treatment and subsequent animal care to the animal's owner. In research and laboratory work, the veterinary technician must record and discuss results among colleagues. In most practical veterinary settings, the veterinary technician must record various information on a computer.

REQUIREMENTS

High School
Veterinary technicians must have a high school diploma. High school students who excel at math and science have a strong foundation on which to build. Those who have had pets or who simply love animals and would like to work with them also fit the profile of a veterinary technician.

Postsecondary Training
The main requirement is the completion of a two- to four-year college-based accredited program. Upon graduation, the student receives an associate's or bachelor's degree. Currently, about 160 veterinary technology programs in 45 states are accredited by the American Veterinary Medical Association (AVMA). A few states do their own accrediting, using the AVMA and associated programs as benchmarks.

Most accredited programs offer thorough course work and preparatory learning opportunities to the aspiring veterinary technician. Typical courses include mathematics, chemistry, humanities, biological science, communications, microbiology, liberal arts, ethics/jurisprudence, and basic computers.

Once the students complete this framework, they move on to more specialized courses. Students take advanced classes in animal nutrition, animal care and management, species/breed identification, veterinary anatomy/physiology, medical terminology, radiography and other clinical procedure courses, animal husbandry, parasitology, laboratory animal care, and large/small animal nursing.

Veterinary technicians must be prepared to assist in surgical procedures. In consideration of this, accredited programs offer surgical nursing courses. In these courses, a student learns to identify and use surgical instruments, administer anesthesia, and monitor animals during and after surgery.

In addition to classroom study, accredited programs offer practical courses. Hands-on education and training are commonly achieved through a clinical practicum, or internship, where the student has the opportunity to work in a clinical veterinary setting. During this period, a student is continuously evaluated by the participating veterinarian and encouraged to apply the knowledge and skills learned.

Certification or Licensing

Although the AVMA determines the majority of the national codes for veterinary technicians, state codes and laws vary. Most states offer registration or certification, and the majority of these states require graduation from an AVMA-accredited program as a prerequisite for taking the National Veterinary Technician Examination or a similar state or local examination. Most colleges and universities assist graduates with registration and certification arrangements. To keep abreast of new technology and applications in the field, practicing veterinary technicians may be required to complete a determined number of annual continuing education courses. The American Association for Laboratory Animal Science offers certification to veterinary technicians who are interested in working in research settings. The American Association of Equine Veterinary Technicians and Assistants and the Academy of Veterinary Emergency and Critical Care Technicians also offer certification.

Other Requirements

As a veterinarian technician, you should be able to meet, talk, and work well with a variety of people. An ability to communicate with the animal owner is as important as diagnostic skills.

In clinical or private practice, it is usually the veterinary technician who conveys and explains treatment and subsequent animal care to the animal's owner. Technicians may have to help euthanize (that is, humanely kill) an animal that is very sick or severely injured and cannot get well. As a result, they must be emotionally stable and help pet owners deal with their grief and loss.

EXPLORING

High school students can acquire exposure to the veterinary field by working with animals in related settings. For example, a high school student may be able to work as a part-time animal attendant or receptionist in a private veterinary practice. Paid or volunteer positions may be available at kennels, animal shelters, and training schools. However, direct work with animals in a zoo is unlikely for high school students.

EMPLOYERS

Approximately 79,600 veterinary technicians and technologists are employed in the United States. Veterinary technicians work for veterinary clinics and animal hospitals, zoos, schools and universities, and animal training programs. In rural areas, farmers hire veterinary technicians as well as veterinarians. Jobs for veterinary technicians in zoos are relatively few, since there are only a certain number of zoos across the country. Those veterinary technicians with an interest in research should seek positions at schools with academic programs for medical science or veterinary medicine. The majority of veterinary technicians find employment in animal hospitals or private veterinary practices, which exist all over the country. However, there are more job opportunities for veterinary technicians in more densely populated areas.

STARTING OUT

Veterinary technicians who complete an accredited program and become certified or registered by the state in which they plan to practice are often able to receive assistance in finding a job through their college's career services offices. Students who have completed internships may receive job offers from the place where they interned.

Veterinary technician graduates may also learn of clinic openings through classified ads in newspapers. Opportunities in zoos and research facilities are usually listed in specific industry periodicals.

ADVANCEMENT

Where a career as a veterinary technician leads is entirely up to the individual. Opportunities are unlimited. With continued education, veterinary technicians can move into allied fields such as veterinary medicine, nursing, medical technology, radiology, and pharmacology. By completing two more years of college and receiving a bachelor's degree, a veterinary technician can become a *veterinary technologist.* Advanced degrees can open the doors to a variety of specialized fields.

EARNINGS

Earnings are generally low for veterinary technicians in private practices and clinics, but pay scales are steadily climbing due to the increasing demand. Better-paying jobs are in zoos and in research. Those fields of practice are very competitive (especially zoos) and only a small percentage of highly qualified veterinary technicians are employed in them.

Most veterinary technicians are employed in private or clinical practice and research. The U.S. Department of Labor (DOL) reports that the median annual salary for veterinary technicians and technologists was $29,280 in 2009. The lowest paid 10 percent made less than $20,180 annually, and the highest paid 10 percent made more than $43,080 annually. Earnings vary depending on practice setting, geographic location, level of education, and years of experience. Benefits vary and depend on each employer's policies.

WORK ENVIRONMENT

Veterinary technicians generally work 40-hour weeks, although some technicians work more than 50 hours a week. These hours may include a few long weekdays, night shifts, and alternated or rotated Saturdays. Hours may fluctuate, as veterinary technicians may need to have their schedules adjusted to accommodate emergency work. A veterinary technician must be prepared for emergencies. In field or farm work, they often have to overcome weather conditions while treating the animal. Injured animals can be very dangerous, and veterinary technicians have to exercise extreme caution when caring for them. A veterinary technician also handles animals that are diseased or infested with parasites. Some of these conditions, such as ringworm, are contagious, so the veterinary technician must understand how these conditions are transferred to humans and take precautions to prevent the spread of diseases.

People who become veterinary technicians care about animals. For this reason, maintaining an animal's well-being or helping to cure an ill animal is very rewarding work. In private practice, technicians get to know the animals they care for. This provides the opportunity to actually see the animals' progress. In other areas, such as zoo work, veterinary technicians work with very interesting, sometimes endangered, species. This work can be challenging and rewarding in the sense that they are helping to save a species and continuing efforts to educate people about these animals. Veterinary technicians who work in research gain satisfaction from knowing their work contributes to promoting both animal and human health.

OUTLOOK

Employment for veterinary technicians will grow much faster than the average for all other occupations through 2018, according to the DOL. Veterinary medicine is a field that is not adversely affected by the economy, so it does offer stability. The public's love for pets coupled with higher disposable incomes will encourage continued demand for workers in this occupation. There should be strong opportunities for veterinary technicians in biomedical facilities, humane societies, animal control facilities, diagnostic laboratories, wildlife facilities, drug or food manufacturing companies, and food safety inspection facilities. Veterinary technicians who assist veterinarians who treat farm animals will also be in strong demand. Competitions for jobs in aquariums and zoos is expected to be very strong as a result of low turnover, the attractiveness of these positions, and slow growth in the construction of new facilities.

FOR MORE INFORMATION

For more information on careers, schools, and resources, contact the following organizations:

Academy of Veterinary Emergency and Critical Care Technicians
6335 Camp Bullis Road, Suite 12
San Antonio, TX 78257-9721
Tel: 210-826-1488
http://avecct.org

American Association for Laboratory Animal Science
9190 Crestwyn Hills Drive
Memphis, TN 38125-8538
Tel: 901-754-8620
E-mail: info@aalas.org
http://www.aalas.org

American Association of Equine Veterinary Technicians and Assistants
http://www.aaevt.org

American Veterinary Medical Association
1931 North Meacham Road, Suite 100
Schaumburg, IL 60173-4360
Tel: 800-248-2862
http://www.avma.org

Association of Zoo Veterinary Technicians
http://www.azvt.org

National Association of Veterinary Technicians in America
1666 K Street, NW, Suite 260
Washington, DC 20006-1260
Tel: 888-996-2882
http://www.navta.net

For information on veterinary careers in Canada, contact
Canadian Veterinary Medical Association
339 Booth Street
Ottawa, ON K1R 7K1 Canada
Tel: 613-236-1162
E-mail: admin@cvma-acmv.org
http://www.canadianveterinarians.net

INTERVIEW

Shelley Harpster is a registered veterinary technician and the registrar at the Great Plains Zoo in Sioux Falls, South Dakota. She discussed her career with the editors of Careers in Focus: Animal Care.

Q. Why did you decide to enter this career?

A. My original career goal was to be a veterinarian. I started out attending a technical college for veterinary technicians, started working as a veterinary technician, and decided that I enjoyed this part of veterinary medicine (being a technician) and not go on to be a veterinarian.

Q. What are your main and secondary job duties?

A. My main job duty is to assist our veterinarian in the treatment of all zoo animals. My secondary job duties include caring for quarantined animals, assisting the keepers in their duties, and record keeping for the animal collection.

Q. How did you train for this career? What was your educational path?

A. My training for this career started when I was a child as a pet owner. My family had a dog that was my responsibility. It was my responsibility to feed and clean up after him every day. I also did his obedience training.

After graduating from high school, I attended a private technical college that offered a veterinary technician program. I also participated in a three-month internship with a private equine-only practice.

Q. How/where did you get your first job in this field?

A. My first job was at my internship practice; it was a part-time graveyard shift. My first full-time job was at a small animal practice. I was hired by a small animal practice after I sent out my resume and personalized cover letters to all of the veterinary practices in the area where I lived.

I found my first job as a zoo veterinary technician by visiting a local zoo's Web site. The timing was perfect; they happened to be hiring their first veterinary technician.

Q. What advice would you give to high school students who are interested in this career?

A. Take as many science and math classes as possible! Be proud of the profession you choose and do your job proudly.

Q. What are some of the pros and cons of work in this field?

A. This is not a very high-paying profession, but it is very rewarding. Being able to help with the treatment of a sick or injured animal is very rewarding when the treatment works and very saddening when it doesn't work. Working in zoos provides many challenges that are not seen when dealing with domestic animals such as not being able to handle/examine many of your patients unless they are sedated. Sometimes the working conditions are not comfortable—especially in the middle of the winter in South Dakota. The biggest pro is that I am the coolest aunt/mother/friend ever because I work in a zoo!

Pros: challenging, rewarding when treatments go well, animals begin to recognize you (this can be good or bad), able to educate the public on conservation issues, working outside (summer), coolest job ever!

Cons: Challenging, it is still sad to lose a favorite animal, working outside (winter), unable to hold/pet your patients.

Zoo and Aquarium Curators and Directors

OVERVIEW

Zoos are wild kingdoms, and aquariums are underwater worlds. The word *zoo* comes from the Greek for "living being" and is a shortened term for zoological garden or zoological park; although this may imply that zoos are created just for beauty and recreation, the main functions of modern zoos are education, conservation, and the study of animals. The term *aquarium* comes from the Latin for "source of water"; in such places, living aquatic plants and animals are studied and exhibited. These land and water gardens are tended by people with an affinity for animals.

Zoo and aquarium curators are the chief employees responsible for the care of the creatures found at these public places; they oversee the various sections of the animal collections, such as birds, mammals, and fishes. There are approximately 11,700 curators employed in the United States. Only a small percentage of this total work at zoos and aquariums.

Zoo and aquarium directors, or *chief executive officers,* are administrators who coordinate the business affairs of these centers. Directors execute the institution's policies, usually under the direction of a governing authority. They are responsible for the institution's operations and plans for future development and for such tasks as fund-raising and public relations. They also serve as representatives of, and advocates for, their institutions and their entire industry.

HISTORY

Prehistoric humans did not try to tame animals; for purposes of survival, they hunted them to avoid danger as well as to obtain food. The full history of the establishment of zoos and aquariums can be traced probably as far back as the earliest attempts by humans to domesticate animals after realizing that they could live with them as fellow creatures. The precise timing of this phenomenon is not known; it apparently occurred at different times in different parts of the world.

Ancient Sumerians kept fish in manmade ponds around 4,500 years ago. By 1150 B.C., pigeons, elephants, antelope, and deer were held captive for taming in such areas as the Middle East, India, and China. In 1000 B.C., a Chinese emperor named Wen Wang built a zoo and called it the Garden of Intelligence. Also around this time, the Chinese and Japanese were breeding and raising goldfish and carp for their beauty.

Zoos were abundant in ancient Greece; animals were held in captivity for purposes of study in nearly every city-state. In early Egypt and Asia, zoos were created mainly for public show, and during the Roman Empire, fish were kept in ponds and animals were collected both for arena showings and for private zoos. A fantastic zoo, with 300 keepers taking care of birds, mammals, and reptiles, was created in Mexico in the early 16th century by Hernando Cortes, the Spanish conqueror.

Zoo and aquarium professions as we know them today began to be established around the mid-18th century with the construction of various extravagant European zoos. The Imperial Menagerie of the Schönbrunn Zoo in Vienna, Austria, was opened in 1765 and still operates to this day. One of the most significant openings occurred in 1828 at the London Zoological Society's Regent's Park. The world's first public aquarium was also established at Regent's Park, in 1853, after which aquariums were built in other European cities. In the United States, P. T. Barnum was the first to establish a display aquarium, which opened in New York in 1856.

Of the aquariums located in most large cities throughout the world, the largest research facilities include the Oceanographic Institute (Monaco) and the Scripps Institution of Oceanography (California). Commercial aquariums include Sea World (Orlando, Florida; San Diego, California; and San Antonio, Texas) and the Miami Seaquarium (Florida), which show fish in tanks that hold as much as 1 million gallons of water.

Today's zoos and aquariums are built around habitat-based, multi-species exhibits designed to immerse the visitor in an experience

Learn More About It

Brazaitis, Peter. *You Belong in a Zoo!: Tales from a Lifetime Spent with Cobras, Crocs, and Other Extraordinary Creatures.* New York: Villard, 2004.

Fisher, Lester E. *Dr. Fisher's Life on the Ark: Green Alligators, Bushman, and Other "Hare-Raising" Tales from America's Most Popular Zoo and Around the World.* Ashland, Ohio: Racom Communications, 2004.

Hosey, Geoff, Vicky Melfi, and Sheila Pankhurst. *Zoo Animals: Behaviour, Management and Welfare.* New York: Oxford University Press, USA, 2009.

Nyhuis, Allen W., and Jon Wassner. *America's Best Zoos: A Travel Guide for Fans & Families.* Branford, Conn.: The Intrepid Traveler, 2008.

Van Tuyl, Christine. *Zoos and Animal Welfare.* Farmington Hills, Mich.: Greenhaven Press, 2007.

simulating a visit to the wild places from which the animals came. The keeping and breeding of captive animals is no longer an end in itself, but a means of educating and communicating a strong conservation imperative to the public. The public has embraced this change, with visitor numbers rising steadily each year.

Along with this expanded public role has come a professionalization of the industry, marked by advances in animal husbandry, veterinary care, nutrition, and exhibit technology that have greatly improved the conditions under which animals are held. These advances have been costly, and the rise in operating expenses reflects these increased costs. Zoos and aquariums today are big business.

Today, curators have a host of responsibilities involved with the operation of zoos and aquariums. Although many zoos and aquariums are separate places, there are also zoos that contain aquariums as part of their facilities. There are both public and private institutions, large and small, and curators often contribute their knowledge to the most effective methods of design, maintenance, and administration for these institutions.

The director's job has changed radically in the past 15 years, reflecting the overall maturity of the zoo and aquarium business. Directors no longer have direct responsibility for working with animals or managing the people who care for them. The director's role has broadened from animal management to overall management, with a focus that has shifted from the day-to-day details of running the facility to ensuring the ongoing success of the entire operation.

THE JOB

General curators of zoos and aquariums oversee the management of an institution's entire animal collection and animal management staff. They help the director coordinate activities, such as education, collection planning, exhibit design, new construction, research, and public services. They meet with the director and other members of the staff to create long-term strategic plans. General curators may have public relations and development responsibilities, such as meeting with the media and identifying and cultivating donors. In most institutions, general curators develop policy; other curators implement policy.

Animal curators are responsible for the day-to-day management of a specific portion of a zoo's or aquarium's animal collection (as defined taxonomically, such as mammals or birds, or ecogeographically, such as the tidal pool); the people charged with caring for that collection, including assistant curators, zookeepers, administrative staff such as secretaries, as well as researchers, students, and volunteers; and the associated facilities and equipment.

For example, the curator in charge of the marine mammal department of a large zoo would be responsible for the care of such animals as sea lions, dolphins, manatees, polar bears, sea and marine otters, and walrus. He or she might oversee more than 100 animals, representing nearly 120 different species, manage scores of employees, and have a multimillion dollar budget.

Assistant curators report to curators and assist in animal management tasks and decisions. They may have extensive supervisory responsibilities.

Curators have diverse responsibilities and their activities vary widely from day to day. They oversee animal husbandry procedures, including the daily care of the animals, establish proper nutritional programs, and manage animal health delivery in partnership with the veterinary staff. They develop exhibits, educational programs, and visitor services and participate in research and conservation activities. They maintain inventories of animals and other records, and they recommend and implement acquisitions and dispositions of animals. Curators serve as liaisons with other departments.

Curators prepare budgets and reports. They interview and hire new workers. When scientific conferences are held, curators attend them as representatives of the institutions for which they work. They are often called upon to write articles for scientific journals and perhaps provide information for newspaper reports and magazine stories. They may coordinate or participate in on-site research or conservation efforts. To keep abreast with developments in their field, curators spend a lot of time reading.

Curators meet with the general curator, the director, and other staff to develop the objectives and philosophy of the institution and decide on the best way to care for and exhibit the animals. They must be knowledgeable about the animals' housing requirements, daily care, medical procedures, dietary needs, and social and reproduction habits. Curators represent their zoos or aquariums in collaborative efforts with other institutions, such as the more than 110 Association of Zoos and Aquariums (AZA) Species Survival Plans that target individual species for intense conservation efforts by zoos and aquariums. In this capacity, curators may exchange information, negotiate breeding loans, or assemble the necessary permits and paperwork to effect the transfers. Other methods of animal acquisition coordinated by curators involve purchases from animal dealers or private collectors and collection of nonendangered species from the wild. Curators may arrange for the quarantine of newly acquired animals. They may arrange to send the remains of dead animals to museums or universities for study.

Curators often work on special projects. They may serve on multidisciplinary committees responsible for planning and constructing new exhibits. Curators interface with colleagues from other states and around the world in collaborative conservation efforts.

Although most zoo and aquarium curators check on the collection on a regular basis, they are usually more involved with administrative issues than animal husbandry. Much of their time is spent in meetings or writing e-mails or on talking on the phone.

In addition to animal curators, large institutions employ curators whose responsibilities involve areas other than animal husbandry, such as research, conservation, exhibits, horticulture, and education.

Working under the supervision of a governing board, directors are charged with pulling together all the institution's operations, development of long-range planning, implementation of new programs, and maintenance of the animal collection and facilities. Much of the director's time is spent meeting with the volunteer governing board and with departmental staff who handle the institution's daily operations.

Directors plan overall budgets; this includes consideration of fund-raising programs, government grants, and private financial support from corporations, foundations, and individuals. They work with the board of directors to design major policies and procedures, and they meet with the curators to discuss animal acquisitions, public education, research projects, and developmental activities. In larger zoos and aquariums, directors may give speeches, appear at fund-raising events, and represent their organizations on television or radio.

A major part of the director's job is seeing that his or her institution has adequate financial resources. Where zoos and aquariums were once funded largely by local and state governments, the amount of tax money available for this purpose is dwindling. Generally, zoos and aquariums need to generate enough revenue to pay for about two-thirds of their operating expenses from sources such as donations, membership, retail sales, and visitor services.

As zoos and aquariums endeavor to improve facilities for animals and visitors alike and to present the conservation message to the public in a more effective manner, renovation of existing structures and construction of new exhibits is an ongoing process. Directors spend much of their time working with architects, engineers, contractors, and artisans on these projects.

Directors are responsible for informing the public about what is going on at the zoo or aquarium. This involves interviews with the media, answering questions from individuals, and even resolving complaints. In addition to being interviewed by journalists and other writers, directors do writing of their own for in-house newsletters and annual reports or for general circulation magazines and newspapers.

Although not directly involved in animal management within his or her own institution, the director may play a significant role in conservation at a regional, national, or international level. Directors work on committees for various conservation organizations, such as AZA Species Survival Plans. They may be involved at a higher level of the AZA, working on such things as accreditation of other institutions, developing professional ethics, or long-range planning. Directors work with other conservation groups as well and may serve in leadership positions for them too.

As zoos and aquariums expand their conservation role from only the management of captive animals to supporting the preservation of the habitats those animals came from, directors are working with universities and field biologists to support research.

Other directorial personnel include *assistant directors* and *deputy directors*. Like curators, these workers are responsible for a specific duty or department, such as operations, education, or animal management. They also manage certain employees, supervise animal care workers, and take care of various administrative duties to help the director.

A bird curator (right) and senior zookeeper place flamingo eggs into a cooler in preparation for transport to another zoo. *(Lynne Sladky, AP Photo)*

REQUIREMENTS

High School

High school students who want to prepare for careers in upper management in zoos and aquariums should take classes in the sciences, especially biology, microbiology, chemistry, and physics, as well as in mathematics, computer science, business, language, and speech.

Extracurricular activities for students interested in becoming zoo and aquarium curators and directors should focus on developing leadership and communication skills: these include student body associations, service clubs, debate teams, and school newspapers.

Postsecondary Training

The minimum formal educational requirement for curators is a bachelor's degree in one of the biological sciences, such as zoology, ecology, biology, oceanography, mammalogy, and ornithology. Course work should include biology, invertebrate zoology, vertebrate physiology, comparative anatomy, organic chemistry, physics, microbiology, and virology. Electives are just as important, particularly writing, public speaking, computer science, and education. Even studying a second language can be helpful.

Typically, an advanced degree is required for curators employed at most institutions—many curators are required to have a doctoral degree. But advanced academic training alone is insufficient; it takes years of on-the-job experience to master the practical aspects of exotic animal husbandry. Also required are management skills, supervisory experience, writing ability, research experience, and sometimes the flexibility to travel.

A few institutions offer curatorial internships designed to provide practical experience. Several major zoos offer formal keeper training courses as well as on-the-job training programs to students who are studying areas related to animal science and care. Such programs could lead to positions as assistant curators. Contact the AZA for further information about which schools and animal facilities are involved in internship programs.

A director's education and experience must be rather broad, with a solid foundation in animal management skills. Therefore, a good balance between science and business is the key to finding a position in this field. Directors need courses in zoology or biology as well as business courses, such as economics, accounting, and general business, and humanities, such as sociology.

Today, most directors have a master's degree; many at larger institutions have doctoral degrees. Directors continue their education throughout their careers by taking classes as well as by reading and learning on their own.

Other Requirements

Curators who work for zoos and aquariums must have a fondness and compassion for animals. But as managers of people, strong interpersonal skills are extremely important for curators, including conflict management and negotiating. Curators spend a lot of time making deals with people inside and outside of their institutions. They must have recognized leadership ability, good coaching skills, and the ability to create and maintain a team atmosphere and build consensus.

Curators also need excellent oral and written communication skills. They must be effective and articulate public speakers. They need to be good at problem solving.

Curators should have an in-depth knowledge of every species and exhibit in their collections and how they interact. Modern zoo and aquarium buildings contain technologically advanced, complex equipment, such as environmental controls, and often house mixed-species exhibits. Not only must curators know about zoology and animal husbandry, but they must understand the infrastructure as well.

Zoo and aquarium directors are leaders and communicators. Inspiring others and promoting their institution are among their most important tasks. Their most important traits include leadership ability, personal charisma, people skills, and public speaking ability.

Directors need to be politically savvy. They interact with many different groups, each with their own agendas. They must be able to build bridges between these various groups and put together a consensus. They need to be flexible and open-minded without losing sight of their role as advocate for their institution. Directors must have outstanding time management skills, and they must be willing and able to delegate.

Directors must be articulate and sociable. They must be able to communicate effectively with people from all walks of life. Much of their time is spent cultivating prospective donors. They must be comfortable with many different types of people, including those with wealth and power.

EXPLORING

Reading about animals or surfing the Internet, taking classes at local zoos and aquariums, or joining clubs, such as 4-H or Audubon, can help students learn about animals. Taking time to learn about ecology and nature in general will prepare students for the systems-oriented approach used by modern zoo and aquarium managers.

Volunteering at zoos or aquariums, animal shelters, wildlife rehabilitation facilities, stables, or veterinary hospitals demonstrates a serious commitment to animals and provides firsthand experience with them.

Professional organizations, such as AZA and the American Association of Zoo Keepers, Inc. (AAZK), have special membership rates for nonprofessionals. Associate members receive newsletters and can attend workshops and conferences.

The AZA offers practical advice for students who are considering animal facility jobs such as that of the director. Suggestions for exploration include visiting zoos and aquariums and learning how they operate, trying to decide on a specific interest, attending events and meetings planned by zoos and aquariums in your area, and continuing to read books and journals on animals and nature.

EMPLOYERS

Approximately 11,700 curators are employed in the United States. Only a small percentage of this total work at zoos and aquariums.

Zoos and aquariums are found throughout the United States, but the largest facilities are located in big cities or areas that have high tourist traffic.

STARTING OUT

Neither the position of zoo and aquarium curator nor the position of director is an entry-level job. Although there are exceptions, most curators start their careers as zookeepers or aquarists and move up through the animal management ranks.

Although the competition for zoo and aquarium jobs is intense, there are several ways to pursue such positions. Getting an education in animal science is a good way to make contacts that may be valuable in a job search. Professors and school administrators often can provide advice and counseling on finding jobs as a curator. The best sources for finding out about career opportunities at zoos and aquariums are trade journals (AZA's *Connect Magazine* or AAZK's *Animal Keepers' Forum),* the Web sites of specific institutions, and special-focus periodicals. Most zoos and aquariums have internal job postings. A few zoos and aquariums have job lines. People in the profession often learn about openings by word of mouth.

Working on a part-time or volunteer basis at an animal facility could provide an excellent opportunity to improve eligibility for higher level jobs in later years. Although many curators have worked in other positions in different fields before obtaining their jobs at animal facilities, others began their careers in lower level jobs at such places and worked their way up to where they wanted to be.

Moving up from a supervisory keeper position to a curatorial job usually involves moving out to another institution, often in another city or state.

Today's zoo and aquarium directors often are people who began their careers in education, marketing, business, research, and academia as well as animal management.

ADVANCEMENT

Curatorial positions are often the top rung of the career ladder for many zoo and aquarium professionals. Curators do not necessarily wish to become zoo or aquarium directors, although the next step for specialized curators is to advance to the position of general curator. Those who are willing to forego direct involvement with animal management altogether and complete the transition to the business of running a zoo or aquarium will set as their ultimate goal the position of zoo or aquarium director. Curators who work for a small facility may aspire to a curatorial position at a larger zoo or aquarium, with greater responsibilities and a commensurate increase in pay.

Advancing to executive positions requires a combination of experience and education. General curators and zoo directors often have graduate degrees in zoology or in business or finance. Continuing professional education, such as AZA's courses in applied zoo and aquarium biology, conservation education, institutional record keeping, population management, and professional management, can be helpful. Attending workshops and conferences sponsored by professional groups or related organizations and making presentations is another means of networking with colleagues from other institutions and professions and becoming better known within the zoo world.

EARNINGS

Salaries of zoo and aquarium curators and directors vary widely depending on factors including the size and location of the institution, whether it is privately or publicly owned, the size of its endowments and budget, and job responsibilities, educational background, and experience. Generally, zoos and aquariums in metropolitan areas pay higher salaries.

The median annual salary for all curators was $47,930 in 2009, according to the U.S. Department of Labor. Salaries ranged from less than $27,000 to $83,900 or more.

Directors tend to be the highest paid employees at zoos and aquariums; the range of their salary is also broad, from $30,000 to more than $100,000 per year, with some directors at major institutions earning considerably more than $150,000. Given the scope of their responsibilities, salaries are not very high.

Most zoos and aquariums provide benefits packages including medical insurance, paid vacation and sick leave, and generous retirement benefits. As salaried employees, curators and directors are not eligible for overtime pay, but they may get compensatory time for extra hours worked. Larger institutions may also offer coverage for prescription drugs, dental and vision insurance, mental health plans, and retirement savings plans. Private corporate zoos may offer better benefits, including profit sharing.

WORK ENVIRONMENT

The work atmosphere for curators and directors of animal facilities will always center on the zoo or aquarium in which they work.

Curators spend most of their time indoors at their desks, reading e-mail, talking on the phone, writing reports, meeting deadlines for budgets, planning exhibits, and so forth. Particularly at large institutions, the majority of their time is spent on administrative duties rather than hands-on interaction with animals. Like other zoo and aquarium employees, curators often work long hours tending to the varied duties to which they are assigned.

When the unexpected happens, curators get their share of animal emergencies. In difficult situations, they may find themselves working late into the night with keepers and veterinarians to help care for sick animals or those that are giving birth.

Directors tend to spend a great deal of time in their offices conducting business affairs. They attend a lot of meetings.

Curators and directors are sometimes required to travel to conferences and community events. They might also travel to other institutions throughout the country or abroad to attend meetings of professional organizations and conservation groups or to discuss animal transfers and other matters. Often, curators and directors lead groups on trips around the United States or to developing countries.

Despite the tedium and the long hours, zoo and aquarium curators and directors derive great personal satisfaction from their work.

OUTLOOK

There are only about 215 professionally operated zoos, aquariums, wildlife parks, and oceanariums in North America. Considering the number of people interested in animal careers, this is not a large number. Therefore, it is expected that competition for jobs as curators and directors (as well as for most zoo and aquarium jobs) will continue to be very strong.

Because there are so few zoos and aquariums in the country, most positions will be the result of turnover, which is low. While a few new zoos and aquariums may open and others may expand their facilities, the number of new curator positions available will be extremely low, particularly compared to the number of interested job seekers. The number of curators and directors employed by each facility depends upon the size and budget of the operation and the range of animal types they house.

The employment outlook for zoo curators and directors is not favorable. Because of the slow growth in new zoos and in their capacity to care for animals, job openings are not expected to grow rapidly. The prospects for aquarium curators and directors is somewhat better due to planned construction of several new aquariums.

However, competition and low turnover rates will continue to squelch opportunities in these occupations. One area with greater growth potential than conventional zoos and aquariums is privately funded conservation centers.

FOR MORE INFORMATION

Visit the alliance's Web site for information on marine mammals, internships, and publications.

Alliance of Marine Mammal Parks and Aquariums
E-mail: ammpa@aol.com
http://www.ammpa.org

For information on membership, a list of accredited zoos throughout the world, and careers in aquatic and marine science, including job listings, contact

Association of Zoos and Aquariums
8403 Colesville Road, Suite 710
Silver Spring, MD 20910-3314
Tel: 301-562-0777
http://www.aza.org

Zookeepers

QUICK FACTS

School Subjects
Biology
Computer science
Speech

Personal Skills
Helping/teaching
Technical/scientific

Work Environment
Indoors and outdoors
Primarily one location

Minimum Education Level
Bachelor's degree

Salary Range
$15,080 to $19,550 to
$40,000+

Certification or Licensing
None available

Outlook
More slowly than the average

DOT
412

GOE
03.02.01

NOC
6483

O*NET-SOC
39-2021.00

OVERVIEW

Zookeepers provide the day-to-day care for animals in zoological parks. They prepare the diets, clean and maintain the exhibits and holding areas, and monitor the behavior of animals that range from the exotic and endangered to the more common and domesticated. Zookeepers interact with visitors and conduct formal and informal educational presentations. They sometimes assist in research studies and may also train animals, depending on the species.

HISTORY

Humans have put wild animals on display since ancient times. About 1500 B.C., Queen Hatshepsut of Egypt established the earliest known zoo. Five hundred years later, the Chinese emperor Wen Wang founded a zoo that covered about 1,500 acres. Rulers seeking to display their wealth and power established small zoos in northern Africa, India, and China. The ancient Greeks established public zoos, while the Romans had many private zoos. During the Middle Ages, from about A.D. 400 to 1500, zoos became rare in Europe.

By the end of the 1400s, European explorers returned from the New World with strange animals, and interest in zoos renewed. During the next 250 years, a number of zoos were established. Some merely consisted of small collections of bears or tigers kept in dismal cages or pits. They were gradually replaced by larger collections of animals that received better care.

In 1752, what is now the oldest zoo, the Schönbrunn, opened in Vienna, Austria. Other European zoos followed. In the United

A zookeeper (left) uses a hose to spray down an Asian elephant at the Denver Zoo. *(David Zalubowski, AP Photo)*

States, the Central Park Zoo in New York City opened in 1864, followed by the Buffalo Zoo in New York in 1870 and Chicago's Lincoln Park Zoo in 1874.

Workers were needed to care for the animals in even the earliest zoos. However, this care probably consisted only of giving the animals food and water and cleaning their cages. Little was known about the needs of a particular species, for if an animal died it could be replaced by another animal from the wild. Few zoos owned more than one or two animals of a rare species, so the keepers did not need to be involved in observations or research on an animal's lifestyle, health, or nutrition.

The modern zoo is a far cry from even the menageries of earlier eras. Today's zoos are still in the entertainment field, but they have assumed three additional roles: conservation, education, and research. Each of these roles has become vital due to the increasing pressures on the world's wildlife.

THE JOB

Zookeepers are responsible for providing the basic care required to maintain the health of the animals in their care. Daily tasks include preparing food by chopping or grinding meat, fish, vegetables, or fruit; mixing prepared commercial feeds; and unbaling forage grasses. Administering vitamins or medications may be necessary as well. In addition, zookeepers fill water containers in the cages. They clean animal quarters by hosing, scrubbing, raking, and disinfecting.

Zookeepers must safely shift animals from one location to another. They maintain exhibits (for example, by planting grass or putting in new bars) and modify them to enhance the visitors' experience. They also provide enrichment devices for the animals, such as ropes for monkeys to swing on or scratching areas for big cats. They regulate environmental factors by monitoring temperature and humidity or water-quality controls and maintaining an inventory of supplies and equipment. They may bathe and groom animals.

Zookeepers must become experts on the species—and the individuals—in their care. They must observe and understand all types of animal behaviors, including courtship, mating, feeding, aggression, sociality, sleeping, moving, and even urination and defecation. Zookeepers must be able to detect even small changes in an animal's appearance or behavior. They must maintain careful records of these observations in a logbook and file daily written or computerized reports. Often, they make recommendations regarding diet or modification of habitats and implement those changes. In addition, they assist the veterinarian in providing treatment to sick animals and may be called upon to feed and help raise infants. Zookeepers may capture or transport animals. When an animal is transferred to another institution, a keeper may accompany it to aid in its adjustment to its new home.

The professional zookeeper works closely with zoo staff on research, conservation, and animal reproduction. Many keepers conduct research projects, presenting their findings in papers or professional journals or at workshops or conferences. Some keepers participate in regional or national conservation plans or conduct field research in the United States and abroad.

Keepers may assist an animal trainer or instructor in presenting animal shows or lectures to the public. Depending on the species, keepers may train animals to shift or to move in a certain way to facilitate routine husbandry or veterinary care. *Elephant keepers,* for example, train their charges to respond to commands to lift their feet so that they may provide proper foot care, including footpad and toenail trims.

Zookeepers must be able to interact with zoo visitors and answer questions in a friendly, professional manner. Keepers may participate in formal presentations for the general public or for special groups.

This involves being knowledgeable about the animals in one's care, the animals' natural habitat and habits, and the role zoos play in wildlife conservation.

Keepers must carefully monitor activity around the animals to discourage visitors from teasing or harming them. They must be able to remove harmful objects that are sometimes thrown into an exhibit and tactfully explain the "no feeding" policy to zoo visitors.

Taking care of animals is hard work. About 85 percent of the job involves custodial and maintenance tasks, which can be physically demanding and dirty. These tasks must be done both indoors and outdoors, in all types of weather. In addition, there is the risk of an animal-inflicted injury or disease. Although direct contact with animals is limited and strictly managed, the possibility for injury exists when a person is working with large, powerful animals or even small animals that possess sharp teeth and claws.

Because animals require care every day, keepers must work weekends and holidays. They also may be called upon to work special events outside their normal working hours.

In large zoological parks, keepers often work with a limited collection of animals. They may be assigned to work specifically with just one taxonomy, such as primates, large cats, or birds, or with different types of animals from a specific ecogeographic area, such as the tropical rainforest or Africa. In smaller zoos, keepers may have more variety and care for a wider range of species.

REQUIREMENTS

High School

If you're planning a career in zookeeping, take as many science classes while in high school as possible. A broad-based science education including courses in biology, ecology, chemistry, physics, and botany, coupled with mathematics and computer science, will be helpful. Courses in English and speech will help you develop your vocabulary and hone your public speaking skills.

Postsecondary Training

Although practical experience may sometimes be substituted for formal education, most entry-level positions require a four-year college degree. Animal management has become a highly technical and specialized field. Zookeepers do much more than care for animals' bodily comforts: many of today's zookeepers are trained zoologists. They must be able to perform detailed behavioral observations, record keeping, nutrition studies, and health care. Their increased responsibilities make their role an essential one in maintaining a healthy animal collection.

Degrees in animal science, zoology, marine biology, conservation biology, wildlife management, and animal behavior are preferred. Electives are just as important, particularly writing, public speaking, computer science, education, and even foreign languages. Applicants with interdisciplinary training sometimes have an advantage. A few colleges and junior colleges offer a specialized curriculum for zookeepers. Those seeking advancement to curatorial, research, or conservation positions may need a master's degree. Animal care experience such as zoo volunteer, farm or ranch worker, or veterinary hospital worker is a must.

Smaller zoos may hire keeper trainees, who receive on-the-job training to learn the responsibilities of the zookeeper. Several major zoos offer formal keeper training courses, as well as on-the-job training programs, to students who are studying areas related to animal science and care. Contact the Association of Zoos and Aquariums (AZA) for further information about which schools and animal facilities are involved in internship programs. Such programs could lead to full-time positions.

Many institutions offer unpaid internships for high school and college students interested in investigating a career in animal care. Internships may involve food preparation, hands-on experience with the animal collection, interpretive services for the public, exhibit design and construction, or the collection and analysis of data. The length of the internships varies. The minimum age for most of these programs is 18.

Other Requirements

Some zoos require written aptitude tests or oral exams. Applicants must pass a physical exam, as keepers must be physically able to do such demanding work as lifting heavy sacks of feed or moving sick or injured animals.

Union membership is more common at publicly operated zoos, but it is on the rise in privately run institutions as well. There is no single zookeepers' union, and a variety of different unions represent the employees at various zoos and aquariums.

Zookeepers must first and foremost have a fondness and empathy for animals. They should enjoy watching and working with them.

The work of the zookeeper is not glamorous. It takes a special kind of dedication to provide care to captive animals that require attention 24 hours a day, 365 days a year.

Keepers need excellent interpersonal skills to work together and to interact with visitors and volunteers. Strong oral and written communication skills are also required. They should be detail-oriented and enjoy paperwork and record keeping.

They must be able to work well independently and as part of a team. Keepers rely on each other to get their jobs done safely. A calm, stable nature, maturity, good judgment, and the ability to adhere to established animal handling and/or safety procedures is essential. Being in a bad mood can interfere with concentration, endangering the keeper and his or her coworkers.

Keepers must have keen powers of observation. Some animals do not exhibit signs of distress or sickness until it is too late to help them. With experience, keepers learn to recognize signals that indicate that an animal is sick.

Due to the physical demands of the job, keepers must be physically fit. Psychological fitness is important too. Zookeepers have to be able to handle the emotional impact when animals with which they have built a relationship go to another institution or die. They cannot be squeamish about handling body wastes or live food items or dealing with sick animals.

EXPLORING

High school students can explore the field of animal care in several ways. They can learn about animals by reading about them and taking classes in biology and zoology. Most zoos have Web sites containing information about the institution and its programs and career opportunities, as well as about the industry in general. Hobbies such as birding expand the knowledge of animals.

Many institutions offer classes about animals and conservation or educational programs, such as Keeper Encounters, where students can learn firsthand what a zookeeper's job is like.

Some have part-time or summer jobs that can give a good overview of how a zoo operates. Many zoos offer volunteer opportunities for teens, such as Explorers or Junior Zookeeper programs, which are similar to programs for adult volunteers but with closer supervision. Most volunteer programs require a specific time commitment. Opportunities vary between institutions and run the gamut from cleaning enclosures to preparing food to handling domesticated animals to conducting tours or giving educational presentations.

Prospective zookeepers can volunteer or work part time at animal shelters, boarding kennels, wildlife rehabilitation facilities, stables, or animal hospitals. They may get a feel for working with animals by seeking employment on a farm or ranch during the summer. Joining a 4-H club also gives a person hands-on experience with animals. Experience with animals is invaluable when seeking a job and provides opportunities to learn about the realities of work in this field.

Professional organizations have special membership rates for nonprofessionals. Reading their newsletters provides an insider's look at what zoo careers are like. Attending local workshops or national conferences offers an opportunity to network and gather information for charting a career path.

EMPLOYERS

There are about 215 professionally operated zoos, aquariums, wildlife parks, and oceanariums in North America. Most facilities are located in or near large population areas.

STARTING OUT

Despite the low pay and challenging working conditions, competition for jobs at zoos is intense. There are many more candidates than available positions. Most zookeepers enjoy their work, and turnover is low. The majority of new jobs result from the need to replace workers who leave the field. A limited number of jobs are created when new zoos open. Entry-level applicants may find it easier to start out in small zoos in smaller communities, where the pay is usually low, and then move on once they have gained some experience. There are many such small-town zoos in the Midwest.

The days when zookeepers were hired off the street and trained on the job are a thing of the past. Today, most institutions require a bachelor's degree. Practical experience working with animals is a must. This experience can involve volunteering at a zoo or wildlife rehabilitation center, caring for animals in a kennel or animal hospital, or working on a farm or ranch.

Part-time work, summer jobs, or volunteering at a zoo increases an applicant's chances of getting full-time employment. Many zoos fill new positions by promoting current employees. An entry-level position, even if it does not involve working directly with animals, is a means of making contacts and learning about an institution's hiring practices.

Zoos that are municipally operated accept applications through municipal civil service offices. At other zoos, application is made directly at the zoo office.

Occasionally zoos advertise for personnel in the local newspapers. Better sources of employment opportunities are trade journals (AZA's *CONNECT* or the American Association of Zoo Keepers Inc.'s *Animal Keepers' Forum)*, the Web sites of specific institutions, or special-interest periodicals. A few zoos even have job lines.

Most zoos have internal job postings. People in the profession often learn about openings by word of mouth. Membership in a professional organization can be helpful when conducting a job search.

ADVANCEMENT

Job advancement in zoos is possible, but the career path is more limited than in some other professions requiring a college degree. The possibility for advancement varies according to a zoo's size and operating policies and an employee's qualifications.

Continuing professional education is a must to keep current on progress in husbandry, veterinary care, and technology, and in order to advance. The AZA offers formal professional courses in applied zoo and aquarium biology, conservation education, elephant management, institutional record keeping, population management, professional management, and studbook keeping. Attending workshops and conferences sponsored by professional groups or related organizations, such as universities or conservation organizations, is another means of sharing information with colleagues from other institutions and professions.

Most zoos have different levels of animal management staff. The most common avenue for job promotion is from keeper to senior keeper to head keeper, then possibly to area supervisor or assistant curator and then curator. On rare occasions, the next step will be to zoo director. Moving up from the senior keeper level to middle and upper management usually involves moving to another institution, often in another city and state.

In addition to participating in daily animal care, the *senior keeper* manages a particular building on the zoo grounds and is responsible for supervising the keepers working in that facility. An *area supervisor* or *assistant curator* works directly with the curators and is responsible for supervising, scheduling, and training the entire keeper force. In major zoological parks, there are head keepers for each curatorial department.

The *curator* is responsible for managing a specific department or section within the zoo, either defined by taxonomy, such as mammals, birds, or reptiles, or by habitat or ecogeography, such as the forest edge or African savannah. The *curator of mammals*, for example, is in charge of all mammals in the collection and supervises all staff who work with mammals. Usually, an advanced degree in zoology and research experience is required to become a curator, as well as experience working as a zookeeper and in zoo management.

Many zookeepers eschew advancement and prefer to remain in work where they have the most direct interaction with and impact on the animals.

EARNINGS

Most people who choose a career as a zookeeper do not do so for the money, but because they feel compassion for and enjoy being around animals.

Salaries vary widely among zoological parks and depend on the size and location of the institution, whether it is publicly or privately owned, the size of its endowments and budget, and whether the zookeepers belong to a union. Generally, the highest salaries tend to be in metropolitan areas and are relative to the applicant's education and responsibilities.

The zookeeper's salary can range from slightly above minimum wage ($7.25 per hour, or $15,080 annually) to more than $40,000 a year, depending on the keeper's background, grade, and tenure and the zoo's location. Certain areas of the country pay higher wages, reflecting the higher cost of living there. City-run institutions, where keepers are lumped into a job category with less-skilled workers, pay less.

Salaried animal caretakers earned an average salary of $19,550 in 2009, according to the U.S. Department of Labor. The top 10 percent earned more than $31,660, and the bottom 10 percent earned less than $15,590 a year.

Most zoos provide benefits packages that include medical insurance, paid vacation and sick leave, and generous retirement benefits. Keepers at larger institutions may also have coverage for prescription drugs, dental and vision insurance, mental health plans, and 401(k) plans. Those who work on holidays may receive overtime pay or comp time. A few institutions offer awards, research grants, and unpaid sabbaticals. Private corporate zoos may offer better benefits, including profit sharing.

WORK ENVIRONMENT

Cleaning, feeding, and providing general care to the animals is a necessity seven days a week, sometimes outdoors and in adverse weather conditions. The zookeeper must be prepared for a varied schedule that may include working weekends and holidays. Sick animals may need round-the-clock care. A large portion of the job involves routine chores for animals that will not express appreciation for the keeper's efforts.

Some of the work may be physically demanding and involve lifting heavy supplies such as bales of hay. The cleaning of an animal's enclosure may be unpleasant and smelly. Between the sounds of the animals and the sounds of the zoo visitors, the work setting may be quite noisy.

The zookeeper may be exposed to bites, kicks, diseases, and possible fatal injury from the animals he or she attends. He or she must practice constant caution because working with animals presents the potential for danger. Even though an animal may have been held in captivity for years or even since birth, it can be frightened, become stressed because of illness, or otherwise revert to its wild behavior. The keeper must know the physical and mental abilities of an animal, whether it be the strength of an ape, the reaching ability of a large cat, or the intelligence of an elephant. In addition, keepers must develop a healthy relationship with the animals in their care by respecting them as individuals and always being careful to observe safety procedures.

Being a zookeeper is an active, demanding job. The tasks involved require agility and endurance, whether they consist of cleaning quarters, preparing food, or handling animals.

Many keepers would agree that the disadvantages of the job are outweighed by the advantages. A chief advantage is the personal gratification of successfully maintaining wild animals, especially rare or endangered species. A healthy, well-adjusted animal collection provides a keeper with a deep sense of satisfaction.

OUTLOOK

Zoos hire more animal keepers than any other classification. But this is still a very small field. For this reason, employment should grow at a slower rate than the average for all occupations through 2018. Each year, there are many more applicants than positions available. Competition for jobs is stiff in the approximately 215 professionally operated zoological parks, aquariums, and wildlife parks in North America. Opportunities arise mainly through attrition, which is lower than in many other professions, or the startup of a new facility.

As the preservation of animal species becomes more complicated, there will be a continuing need for zoo staff to work to preserve endangered wildlife and educate the public about conservation. The demand will increase for well-educated personnel who will be responsible for much more than simply feeding the animals and cleaning their enclosures. Zookeepers will need more knowledge as zoos expand and become more specialized. The amount of knowledge and effort necessary to maintain and reproduce a healthy animal collection will keep zookeepers in the front line of animal care.

Pursuing a job in this area is well worth the effort for those who are dedicated to providing care for rapidly diminishing animal species and educating the public about the fate of endangered animals and the need to preserve their natural habitats.

FOR MORE INFORMATION

Visit the AAZK Web site to read the online pamphlet Zoo Keeping as a Career.

American Association of Zoo Keepers (AAZK)
3601 29th Street, SW, Suite 133
Topeka, KS 66614-2054
Tel: 785-273-9149
http://aazk.org

Visit the AZA Web site to read Zoo and Aquarium Careers *and* Careers in Aquatic and Marine Science.

Association of Zoos and Aquariums (AZA)
8403 Colesville Road, Suite 710
Silver Spring, MD 20910-3314
Tel: 301-562-0777
http://www.aza.org

Zoologists

OVERVIEW

Zoologists are biologists who study animals. They often select a particular type of animal to study, and they may study an entire animal, one part or aspect of an animal, or a whole animal society. There are many areas of specialization from which a zoologist can choose, such as origins, genetics, characteristics, classifications, behaviors, life processes, and distribution of animals.

HISTORY

Human beings have always studied animals. Knowledge of animal behavior was a necessity to prehistoric humans, whose survival depended on their success in hunting. Those early people who hunted to live learned to respect and even revere their prey. The earliest known paintings, located in the Lascaux Caves in France, depict animals, which demonstrates the importance of animals to early humans. Most experts believe that the artists who painted those images viewed the animals they hunted not just as a food source, but also as an important element of spiritual or religious life.

The first important developments in zoology occurred in Greece, where Alcmaeon, a philosopher and physician, studied animals and performed the first known dissections of humans in the sixth century B.C. Aristotle, however, is generally considered to be the first real zoologist. Aristotle, who studied with the great philosopher Plato and tutored the world-conquering Alexander the Great, had the lofty goal of setting down in writing everything that was known in his

QUICK FACTS

School Subjects
Biology
Chemistry
Earth science

Personal Skills
Communication/ideas
Technical/scientific

Work Environment
Indoors and outdoors
Primarily one location

Minimum Education Level
Bachelor's degree

Salary Range
$33,254 to $56,500 to $100,000+

Certification or Licensing
None available

Outlook
About as fast as the average

DOT
041

GOE
02.03.01, 02.03.03

NOC
2121

O*NET-SOC
19-1020.01, 19-1023.00

Learn More About It

Goodall, Jane. *My Life with the Chimpanzees*. Rev. ed. New York: Aladdin, 1996.

Hunter, Malcolm L., David Lindenmayer, and Aram Calhoun. *Saving the Earth as a Career: Advice on Becoming a Conservation Professional*. Hoboken, N.J.: Wiley-Blackwell, 2007.

Mackay, Richard. *The Atlas of Endangered Species*. Berkeley, Calif.: University of California Press, 2008.

McGavin, George C. *Endangered: Wildlife on the Brink of Extinction*. Richmond Hill, ON, Canada: Firefly Books, 2006.

time. In an attempt to extend that knowledge, he observed and dissected sea creatures. He also devised a system of classifying animals that included 500 species, a system that influenced scientists for many centuries after his death. Some scholars believe that Alexander sent various exotic animals to his old tutor from the lands he conquered, giving Aristotle unparalleled access to the animals of the ancient world.

With the exception of important work in physiology done by the Roman physician Galen, the study of zoology progressed little after Aristotle until the middle of the 16th century. Between 1555 and 1700, much significant work was done in the classification of species and in physiology, especially regarding the circulation of blood, which affected studies of both animals and humans. The invention of the microscope in approximately 1590 led to the discovery and study of cells. In the 18th century, Swedish botanist Carl Linnaeus developed the system of classification of plants and animals that is still used.

Zoology continued to develop at a rapid rate, and in 1859, Charles Darwin published *On the Origin of Species,* which promoted the theory of natural selection, revolutionized the way scientists viewed all living creatures, and gave rise to the field of ethology, the study of animal behavior. Since that time, innumerable advances have been made by zoologists throughout the world.

In the past century, the rapid development of technology has changed zoology and all sciences by giving scientists the tools to explore areas that had previously been closed to them. Computers, submersibles, high-definition cameras, Geographic Information Systems technology, satellites, and tremendously powerful microscopes are only a few of the means that modern zoologists have used to bring new knowledge to light. In spite of these advances, however, mysteries remain, questions go unanswered, and species wait to be discovered.

THE JOB

Although zoology is a single specialty within the field of biology, it is a vast specialty that includes many major subspecialties. Some zoologists study a single animal or a category of animals, whereas others may specialize in a particular part of an animal's anatomy or study a process that takes place in many kinds of animals. A zoologist might study single-cell organisms, a particular variety of fish, or the behavior of groups of animals such as elephants or bees.

Many zoologists are classified according to the animals they study. For example, *entomologists* are experts on insects, *ichthyologists* study fish, *herpetologists* specialize in the study of reptiles and amphibians, *mammalogists* focus on mammals, and *ornithologists* study birds. *Embryologists,* however, are classified according to the process that they study. They examine the ways in which animal embryos form and develop from conception to birth.

Within each primary area of specialization there is a wide range of subspecialties. An ichthyologist, for example, might focus on the physiology, or physical structure and functioning, of a particular fish; on a biochemical phenomenon such as bioluminescence in deepsea species; on the discovery and classification of fish; on variations within a single species in different parts of the world; or on the ways in which one type of fish interacts with other species in a specific environment. Others may specialize in the effects of pollution on fish or in finding ways to grow fish effectively in controlled environments in order to increase the supply of healthy food available for human consumption.

Some zoologists are primarily teachers, while others spend most of their time performing original research. Teaching jobs in universities and other facilities are probably the most secure positions available, but zoologists who wish to do extensive research may find such positions restrictive. Even zoologists whose primary function is research, however, often need to do some teaching in the course of their work, and almost everyone in the field has to deal with the public at one time or another.

Students often believe that zoological scientists spend most of their time in the field, observing animals and collecting specimens. In fact, most researchers spend no more than two to eight weeks in the field each year. Zoologists spend much of their time at a computer or on the telephone.

It is often the case that junior scientists spend more time in the field than do senior scientists, who study specimens and data collected in the field by their younger colleagues. Senior scientists spend much of their time coordinating research, directing younger scientists and technicians, and writing grant proposals or soliciting funds in other ways.

Raising money is an extremely important activity for zoologists who are not employed by government agencies or major universities. The process of obtaining money for research can be time-consuming and difficult. Good development skills can also give scientists a flexibility that government-funded scientists do not have. Government money is sometimes available only for research in narrowly defined areas that may not be those that a scientist wishes to study. A zoologist who wants to study a particular area may seek his or her own funding in order not to be limited by government restrictions.

REQUIREMENTS

High School

To prepare for a career in zoology, make sure to get a well-rounded high school education. Although a solid grounding in biology and chemistry is an absolute necessity, you should remember that facility in English will also be invaluable. Writing monographs and articles, communicating with colleagues both orally and in writing, and writing persuasive fund-raising proposals are all activities at which scientists need to excel. You should also read widely, not merely relying on books on science or other subjects that are required by the school. The scientist-in-training should search the library for magazines and journals dealing with areas that are of personal interest. Developing the habit of reading will help prepare you for the massive amounts of reading involved in research and keeping up with latest developments in the field. Computer skills are also essential, since most zoologists not only use the computer for writing, communication, and research, but they also use various software programs to perform statistical analyses.

Postsecondary Training

A bachelor's degree is the minimum requirement to work as a zoologist; advanced degrees are needed for research or administrative work. Academic training, practical experience, and the ability to work effectively with others are the most important prerequisites for a career in zoology.

Other Requirements

Success in zoology requires tremendous effort. It would be unwise for a person who wants to work an eight-hour day to become a zoologist, since hard work and long hours (sometimes 60 to 80 hours per week) are the norm. Also, although some top scientists are paid extremely well, the field does not provide a rapid route to riches. A successful zoologist finds satisfaction in work, not in a paycheck. The personal rewards, however, can be tremendous. The typical zoologist finds his or her work satisfying on many levels.

A successful zoologist is generally patient and flexible. A person who cannot juggle various tasks will have a difficult time in a job that requires doing research, writing articles, dealing with the public, teaching students, soliciting funds, and keeping up with the latest publications in the field. Flexibility also comes into play when funding for a particular area of study ends or is unavailable. A zoologist whose range of expertise is too narrowly focused will be at a disadvantage when there are no opportunities in that particular area. A flexible approach and a willingness to explore various areas can be crucial in such situations, and a too-rigid attitude may lead a zoologist to avoid studies that he or she would have found rewarding.

An aptitude for reading and writing is a must for any zoologist. A person who hates to read would have difficulty keeping up with the literature in the field, and a person who cannot write or dislikes writing would be unable to write effective articles and books. Publishing is an important part of zoological work, especially for those who are conducting research.

EXPLORING

One of the best ways to find out if you are suited for a career as a zoologist is to talk to zoologists and find out exactly what they do. Contact experts in your field of interest. If you are interested in birds, find out whether there is an ornithologist in your area. If there is not, find an expert in some other part of the country. Read books, magazines, and journals to find out who the experts are. Don't be afraid to write or call people and ask them questions.

One good way to meet experts is to attend meetings of professional organizations. If you are interested in fish, locate organizations of ichthyologists by searching in the library or on the Internet. If you can, attend an organization's meeting and introduce yourself to the attendees. Ask questions and learn as much as you can.

Try to become an intern or a volunteer at an organization that is involved in an area that you find interesting. Most organizations have internships, and if you look with determination for an internship, you are likely to find one.

EMPLOYERS

Zoologists are employed by a wide variety of institutions, not just zoos. Many zoologists are teachers at universities and other facilities, where they may teach during the year while spending their summers doing research. A large number of zoologists are researchers; they may be working for nonprofit organizations (requiring grants to fund their work), scientific institutions, or the government. Of course, there are many zoologists who are employed by zoos, aquariums, and museums. While jobs for zoologists exist all over the country, large cities that have universities, zoos, aquariums, and museums will provide far more opportunities for zoologists than in rural areas.

STARTING OUT

Though it is possible to find work with a bachelor's degree, it is likely that you will need to continue your education to advance further in the field. Competition for higher paying, high-level jobs among those with doctoral degrees is fierce; as a result, it is often easier to break into the field with a master's degree than it is with a Ph.D. Many zoologists with their master's degree seek a mid-level job and work toward a Ph.D. part time.

You will be ahead of the game if you have made contacts as an intern or as a member of a professional organization. It is an excellent idea to attend the meetings of professional organizations, which generally welcome students. At those meetings, introduce yourself to the scientists you admire and ask for their help and advice. Do not be shy, but be sure to treat people with respect. Ultimately, it is the way you relate to other people that determines how your career will develop.

ADVANCEMENT

Higher education and publishing are two of the most important means of advancing in the field of zoology. The holder of a Ph.D. will make more money and have a higher status than the holder of a bachelor's or master's degree. The publication of articles and books is important for both research scientists and professors of zoology. A young professor who does not publish cannot expect to become a full professor with tenure, and a research scientist who does not publish the results of his or her research will not become known as an authority in the field. In addition, the publication of a significant work lets everyone in the field know that the author has worked hard and accomplished something worthwhile.

Because zoology is not a career in which people typically move from job to job, people generally move up within an organization. A professor may become a full professor; a research scientist may become known as an expert in the field or may become the head of a department, division, or institution; a zoologist employed by an aquarium or a zoo may become an administrator or head curator. In some cases, however, scientists may not want what appears to be a more prestigious position. A zoologist who loves to conduct and coordinate research, for example, may not want to become an administrator who is responsible for budgeting, hiring and firing, and other tasks that have nothing to do with research.

EARNINGS

A 2009 survey conducted by the National Association of Colleges and Employers determined that holders of bachelor's degrees in biological and life sciences (including zoologists) earned average starting salaries of $33,254.

The median annual wage for zoologists in 2009 was $56,500, according to the U.S. Department of Labor (DOL). Salaries ranged from less than $35,280 to $93,140 or more. Zoologists who were employed by the federal government had mean annual earnings of $72,330.

It is possible for the best and brightest of zoologists to make substantial amounts of money. Occasionally, a newly graduated Ph.D. who has a top reputation may be offered a position that pays $100,000 or more per year, but only a few people begin their careers at such a high level.

The benefits that zoologists receive as part of their employment vary widely. Employees of the federal government or top universities tend to have extensive benefit packages, but the benefits offered by private industry cover a wide range, from extremely generous to almost nonexistent.

WORK ENVIRONMENT

There is much variation in the conditions under which zoologists work. Professors of zoology may teach exclusively during the school year or may both teach and conduct research. Many professors whose school year consists of teaching spend their summers doing research. Research scientists spend some time in the field, but most of their work is done in the laboratory. There are zoologists who spend most of their time in the field, but they are the exceptions to the rule.

Zoologists who do field work may have to deal with difficult conditions. For example, a gorilla expert may have to spend her time in the forests of Rwanda. A shark expert may need to observe his subjects from a shark cage. A marine ornithologist may have to walk the craggy shoreline during brisk weather to observe birds. For most people in the field, however, that aspect of the work is particularly interesting and satisfying.

Zoologists spend much of their time corresponding with others in their field, studying the latest literature, reviewing articles written by their peers, and making and returning phone calls. They also log many hours working with computers, using computer modeling, performing statistical analyses, recording the results of their research, or writing articles and grant proposals.

No zoologist works in a vacuum. Even those who spend much time in the field have to keep up with developments within their specialty. In most cases, zoologists deal with many different kinds of people, including students, mentors, the public, colleagues, representatives of granting agencies, private or corporate donors, reporters, and science writers. For this reason, the most successful members of the profession tend to develop good communication skills.

OUTLOOK

Employment for zoologists is expected to grow about as fast as the average for all careers through 2018, according to the DOL. The field of zoology is relatively small, and competition for good positions—especially research positions—is high. Upper level jobs are further limited by government budget cuts. Growth in the biological sciences should continue in the next decade, spurred partly by the need to analyze and offset the effects of pollution on the environment. Competition will be strongest for those with doctoral degrees. Those with a bachelor's or master's degree will face less competition due to a larger number of available positions—including those in nonscientist jobs related to zoology, such as marketing, sales, publishing, and research management. Individuals who are most successful in the field in the future are likely to be those who are able to diversify. Zoologists with expertise in a variety of animals or animal systems or processes will have strong employment prospects.

FOR MORE INFORMATION

Visit the alliance's Web site for information on marine mammals, internships, and publications.
Alliance of Marine Mammal Parks and Aquariums
E-mail: ammpa@aol.com
http://www.ammpa.org

The Education section of the institute's Web site has information on a number of careers in biology.
American Institute of Biological Sciences
1444 I Street, NW, Suite 200
Washington, DC 20005-6535
Tel: 202-628-1500
http://www.aibs.org

For information on membership, a list of accredited zoos throughout the world, and careers in aquatic and marine science, including job listings, contact
Association of Zoos and Aquariums
8403 Colesville Road, Suite 710
Silver Spring, MD 20910-3314
Tel: 301-562-0777
http://www.aza.org

This is a membership organization for people and organizations that are committed to "conserving and restoring natural ecosystems, focusing on birds, other wildlife, and their habitats for the benefit of humanity and the earth's biological diversity." Visit its Web site for detailed information and illustrations of birds in the United States and an overview of its programs.
National Audubon Society
225 Varick Street, 7th Floor
New York, NY 10014-4396
Tel: 212-979-3000
http://www.audubon.org

The following society publishes the journal Integrative and Comparative Biology, *and it is a good source of information about all areas and aspects of zoology. For more information, contact*
Society for Integrative and Comparative Biology
1313 Dolley Madison Boulevard, Suite 402
McLean, VA 22101-3926

Tel: 800-955-1236
E-mail: SICB@BurkInc.com
http://www.sicb.org

The society seeks to save wildlife and wild lands. Visit its Web site to learn more about programs for teens and to read sample articles from Wildlife Conservation Magazine.

Wildlife Conservation Society
2300 Southern Boulevard
Bronx, NY 10460-1068
Tel: 718-220-5100
http://www.wcs.org

The Wildlife Society *offers* Careers in Wildlife Conservation, *which details more than 10 careers in the field. The publication is available at its Web site, along with information on other publications, student chapters, certification, and membership for college students or anyone who is interested in wildlife conservation and management.*

The Wildlife Society
5410 Grosvenor Lane, Suite 200
Bethesda, MD 20814-2144
Tel: 301-897-9770
E-mail: TWA@wildlife.org
http://joomla.wildlife.org

The association "promotes conservation, preservation, and propagation of animals in both private and public domains." It offers a membership category for those who support its goals.

Zoological Association of America
PO Box 511275
Punta Gorda, FL 33951-1275
Tel: 941-621-2021
E-mail: info@zaa.org
http://www.zaa.org

Index

Entries and page numbers in **bold** indicate major treatment of a topic.

A

AAZK. *See* American Association of Zoo Keepers
Academy of Rural Veterinarians 169
Academy of Veterinary Emergency and Critical Care Technicians 179, 182
Adams Animal Rescue League of the Palm Beaches (West Palm Beach, Florida) 56–58
adoption counselors 46–47. *See also* animal shelter employees
Advancement section, explained 4
AFBF. *See* American Farm Bureau Federation
Alcmaeon 209
Alexander the Great 209–210
ALF. *See* Animal Liberation Front
ALL. *See* American League of Lobbyists
Alliance of Marine Mammal Parks and Aquariums 77, 197, 217
American Academy of Underwater Scientists 107
American Animal Hospital Association 169
American Association for Laboratory Animal Science 30, 34, 39, 179, 182
American Association of Equine Practitioners 170
American Association of Equine Veterinary Technicians and Assistants 179, 182
American Association of Wildlife Veterinarians 167, 170
American Association of Zoo Keepers (AAZK) 77, 193, 208
American Association of Zoo Veterinarians 167, 170
American Beekeeping Federation 98
American College of Veterinary Behaviorists 65, 170
American Farm Bureau Federation (AFBF) 98
American Fisheries Society 107
American Horse Council 78, 88
American Humane Association
  animal activists 6, 10, 12
  animal shelter employees 51, 54, 55

American Institute of Biological Sciences 108, 217
American Kennel Club 15
American League of Lobbyists (ALL) 9, 12
American Pet Products Association 148, 169
American Riding Instructors Association 84, 88
American Society for the Prevention of Cruelty to Animals (ASPCA)
  animal activists 5–6, 10, 13
  animal caretakers 25
  animal handlers 36
  animal shelter employees 45, 55
  pet shop workers 147, 148, 152, 157
American Society of Animal Science 22
American Society of Association Executives & Center for Association Leadership 12
American Society of Farm Managers and Rural Appraisers 98
American Society of Limnology and Oceanography 105, 106, 108
American Society of Naturalists 119–121
American Veterinary Medical Association (AVMA)
  American Board of Veterinary Specialties 165
  animal caretakers 30, 34
  Council on Education 165
  veterinarians 161, 167, 168, 170
  veterinary technicians 178, 183
American Youth Horse Council 88
American Zoo and Aquarium Association 39
animal activists 5–13
  advancement 11
  animal rights activists 5
  animal treatment investigators 8
  animal welfare activists 5
  certification or licensing 9–10
  cruelty investigators 8
  earnings 11
  educational requirements 9
  employers 11
  exploring the field 10
  for more information 12–13
  high school 9
  history 5–6
  humane educators 8